1925530

Achieving QTS

Reflective Reader: Secondary Science

Achieving QTS: Reflective Readers

Reflective Reader
Secondary Science

Gren Ireson and John Twidle

Learning Matters

First published in 2006 by Learning Matters Ltd.

British Library Cataloguing in Publication Data
A CIP record for this book is available from the British Library.

ISBN-10: 1 84445 065 1
ISBN-13: 978 1 84445 065 7

Cover design by Topics – The Creative Partnership
Project management by Deer Park Productions, Tavistock, Devon
Typeset by PDQ Typesetting Ltd
Printed and bound in Great Britain by Bell & Bain Ltd, Glasgow

Learning Matters Ltd
33 Southernhay East
Exeter EX1 1NX
Tel: 01392 215560
Email: info@learningmatters.co.uk
www.learningmatters.co.uk

Contents

Introduction

The *Reflective Reader* series supports the *Achieving QTS* series by providing relevant and topical theory that underpins the reflective learning and practice of primary and secondary ITT trainees.

Each book includes extracts from classic and current publications and documents. These extracts are supported by analysis, pre- and post-reading activities, links to the QTS Standards, a practical implications section, links to other titles in the *Achieving QTS* series and suggestions for further reading.

Integrating theory and practice, the *Reflective Reader* series is specifically designed to encourage trainees and practising teachers to develop the skill and habit of reflecting on their own practice, engaging with relevant theory and identify opportunities to apply theory to improve their teaching skills.

The process of educating individuals is broader than the specific areas of educational theory, research and practice. All humans are educated, socially, politically and culturally. In all but a few cases humans co-exist with other humans and are educated to do so. The position of an individual in society is determined by the nature and quality of the educational process. As a person grows up, emerging from childhood into adulthood, their social and political status is dependent on the educational process. For every task, from eating and sleeping to reading and writing, whether instinctive or learnt, the knowledge and experience gained through the process of education is critical. Humans are educated, consciously and subconsciously, from birth. Education is concerned with the development of individual autonomy, the understanding of which has been generated by educational, sociological, psychological and philosophical theories.

The position of the teacher in this context is ambivalent. In practice each teacher will have some knowledge of theory but may not have had the opportunity to engage with theories that can inform and improve their practice.

In this series, the emphasis is on theory. The authors guide the student to analyse practice within a theoretical framework provided by a range of texts. Through examining why we do what we do and how we do it the reader will be able to relate theory to practice. The series covers primary and secondary professional issues, subject areas and topics. There are also explicit links to Qualifying to Teach Standards (QTS) that will enable both trainees and teachers to improve and develop their subject knowledge.

Each book provides focused coverage of subjects and topics and each extract is accompanied by support material to help trainees and teachers to engage with the extract, draw out the implications for classroom practice and to develop as a reflective practitioner.

While the series is aimed principally at students, it will also be relevant to practitioners in the classroom and staffroom. Each book includes guidance, advice and examples on:

- the knowledge, understanding, theory and practice needed to achieve QTS status;
- how to relate knowledge, theory and practice to a course of study;
- self reflection and analysis through personal responses and reading alone;
- developing approaches to sharing views with colleagues and fellow students.

Readers will develop their skills in relating theory to practice through:

- preparatory reading;
- analysis;
- personal responses;
- practical implications and activities;
- further reading.

Secondary science

This book is written for those undertaking a secondary phase course leading to QTS in science. You may be undertaking a flexible or full-time PGCE or be employed as a graduate teacher in school.

The book is a reflective reader to support your professional development and runs parallel with both *Achieving QTS: Learning and Teaching in Secondary Schools* (second edition) (Ellis, V., 2004, Learning Matters) and *Achieving QTS: Reflective Reader Secondary Professional Studies* (Hoult, S., 2005, Learning Matters). The text aims to engage you with theory and reflection on a series of key topics that you will experience in your practice. Each chapter will consider the case for particular theories, what these theories are about and how they impact upon practice. They are not intended to be a tool kit for practice but are to help you reflect on your practice and consider some of the wider and deeper issues that underpin this.

Each chapter uses a series of challenging extracts from key thinkers in education. It is not possible to cover the whole range of issues in each chapter, and as such the extracts may steer your thinking to certain areas. However, you will be encouraged to consider these critically and reflect and build on your own practice at the same time. The book should serve as a stimulus for reflective writing, whether for a learning journal or a more formal written assignment.

Each chapter has a set of prompts to aid personal reflection and discussion with colleagues about theory, policy and practice in the light of the issues covered. Further reading is provided and the work is referenced to direct your future enquiry.

It is not possible to discuss all educational issues within a book of this size. Selecting the contents has been a difficult decision but it is hoped that the chapters will cover a range of issues to support you towards QTS.

This book will help you to:

- engage with the issues at a theoretical level with reference to key texts in secondary professional studies;
- explore teaching in the secondary stage of education;
- reflect upon your own principles and development as a teacher and consider how this impacts upon your work in the classroom.

Each chapter is structured around the key reflective prompts what, why and how. Each prompt is linked to a short extract. You will:

- read a short analysis of the extract;
- provide a personal response;
- consider the practical implications,

and have links to:

- supporting reading;
- the QTS Standards.

Supplementary material for this book can be found on the Learning Matters website at www.learningmatters.co.uk.

A note on extracts

Where possible, extracts are reproduced in full but of necessity many have had to be cut. References to other sources embedded within the extracts are not included in this book. Please refer to the extract source for full bibliographical information about any of these.

Authors

Gren Ireson is Senior Lecturer and John Twidle Lecturer in Science Education at Loughborough University where they jointly run the PGCE Secondary Science programme. Both John and Gren also teach on the professional studies and Masters programmes in education. Gren Ireson also teaches on undergraduate modules in sciences. Before working in higher education both John and Gren taught in schools (Gren teaching physics, mathematics, electronics and IT; John teaching chemistry and physics), and led departments.

Both Gren and John maintain research interests in science and science education. Gren: teaching and learning secondary school science; teaching and learning relativity and quantum mechanics; quantum philosophy; the science/technology interface; and women in science. John: teaching and learning secondary school science; children's mastery of the concept of conservation of volume in liquids and solids; language in science; and the use of the Internet to support science teaching.

Series editor

Professor Sonia Blandford is Pro-Vice Chancellor (Dean of Education) at Canterbury Christ Church University, one of the largest providers of initial teacher training and professional development in the United Kingdom. Following a successful career as a teacher in primary and secondary schools, Sonia has worked in higher education for nine years. She has acted as an education consultant to ministries of education in Eastern Europe, South America and South Africa and as an adviser to the European Commission, LEAs and schools. She co-leads the Teach First initiative. The author of a range of education management texts, she has a reputation for her straightforward approach to difficult issues. Her publications include: *Middle Management in Schools* (Pearson), *Resource Management in Schools* (Pearson), *Professional Development Manual* (Pearson), *School Discipline Manual* (Pearson), *Managing Special Educational Needs in Schools* (Sage), *Managing Discipline in Schools* (Routledge), *Managing Professional Development in Schools* (Routledge), *Financial Management in Schools* (Optimus), *Remodelling Schools: Workforce Reform* (Pearson) and *Sonia Blandford's Masterclass* (Sage).

Acknowledgements

Every effort has been made to trace the copyright holders and to obtain their permission for use of copyright material. The publisher and authors will gladly receive information enabling them to rectify any error or omission in subsequent editions.

The authors and publisher would like to thank the following for permission to reproduce copyright material:

Ross, K., Larkin, L. and Callaghan, P., *Teaching Secondary Science*, (2000) David Fulton Publishers. Reproduced with kind permission. White, J., *Do Howard Gardner's Multiple Intelligences Add Up?* (2000) University of London Institute of Education. Reproduced with kind permission of University of London Institute of Education; (2001) Kogan Page. Parkinson, J., *The Effective Teaching of Secondary Science,* (1994) Longman. Reprinted by kind permission of Pearson Education Ltd. Bloom, B. S. *Taxonomy of Educational Objectives,* Longman (1956). Reprinted by kind permission. Erickson, G., in Millar, R., Leach, J. and Osborne, J., *Improving Science Education* (2000). Reproduced with kind permission of the Open University Press/McGraw-Hill Publishing Company. Brooks, V., *Assessment in Secondary Schools* (2002). Reproduced with kind permission of the Open University Press/McGraw-Hill Publishing Company. Ratcliffe, M. and Grace, M., *Science Education for Citizenship* (2003). Reproduced with kind permission of the Open University Press/McGraw-Hill Publishing Company. Adey, P. and Shayer, M., *Learning Intelligence* (2002). Reproduced with kind permission of the Open University Press/McGraw-Hill Publishing Company; Osborne, J. (1997) 'Practical Alternatives'. *School Science Review* Vol 78 No. 285. Reprinted with permission. Borrows, P., in Ratcliffe, M. (Ed), *ASE Guide to Secondary Science Education* (1998). Reprinted with permission by Nelson Thornes.

1 Planning for effective learning in science

By the end of this chapter you will have considered and reflected upon:

- **why** it is important to plan lessons in science;
- **what** are lesson objectives;
- **how** to approach the issue of lesson planning.

Linking your learning
Achieving QTS Reflective Reader: Secondary Professional Studies. Hoult, S. (2005)
Chapter 4 Planning for Learning.

Professional Standards for QTS
1.7, 2.1.c, 2.2, 3.1.1, 3.1.2, 3.1.3, 3.1.4, 3.2.1, 3.2.4, 3.3.2c, 3.3.3, 3.3.7, 3.3.8, 3.3.12

Introduction

During a session on the teaching of genetics, a guest lecturer admitted to a group of PGCE trainees that he sometimes adopted a six-step approach to lesson planning: he decided what he was going to do in the last six steps he took before opening the classroom door! Although this approach certainly does not equate in any way to effective lesson planning to be emulated by a beginning teacher, what the trainees could not see were the 30 years' successful teaching experience that the person standing in front of them had behind him. It is not that such teachers fail to plan thoroughly for their lessons, it is that their plans have become internalised through repetition. Nonetheless, what may serve as an effective plan for an experienced teacher, confident in his subject knowledge, who knows his pupils well and what strategies work for them, has all the appropriate apparatus to hand in the laboratory and is familiar with the demands of the National Curriculum or relevant specification, is unlikely to be effective for a trainee. In fact, for someone new to teaching and the process of lesson planning, even the sample provided on the Standards website (DfES, 2006), we would argue, would be totally inadequate in providing adequate guidance. However, this chapter is not intended to serve as a prescriptive treatise on lesson planning, it is intended to serve more as an awareness-raising exercise in which some of the more important aspects of planning are considered.

Why

There is no single correct way of planning a successful lesson. What works for one teacher may not work for another and, although meticulous planning can result in a technically proficient teacher, becoming a successful teacher requires additional strengths such as subject knowledge, communication skills and the ability to relate to pupils.

As a trainee teacher, preparing your first lessons can be a daunting process involving hours of background reading, gazing at blank sheets of paper, drafting and redrafting of lesson plans.

In order to achieve Qualified Teacher Status (QTS), amongst other professional standards (DfES, 2002), trainees are required to demonstrate (3.1.1) that:

> They set challenging teaching and learning objectives which are relevant to all pupils in their classes. They base these on their knowledge of:
> - the pupils
> - evidence of their past and current achievement
> - the expected standards for pupils of the relevant age range
> - the range and content of work relevant to pupils in that age range.

In addition (3.1.2), trainees should:

> use these teaching and learning objectives to plan lessons, and sequence lessons, showing how they will assess pupils' learning. They take account of and support pupils' varying needs so that girls and boys, from all ethnic groups can make good progress.

Although trainee teachers are compelled to set objectives and prepare lessons, we would hope that this would be done as a matter of good practice even if the compulsion were not there, as we believe that there are irrefutable arguments in favour of such practice.

First and foremost, teaching should be a logical and intentional activity. If this assumption is not accepted then it paints teaching as an aimless, woolly process, staffed by individuals entering the classroom with the hope that something meaningful, and possibly useful, will happen during the lesson. It is therefore important to plan in advance exactly what the outcome of a lesson is intended to be. What is it that you expect your pupils to be able to do by the end of your lesson that they could not do before; what skills should they develop as a result of your teaching; what additional knowledge should they have gained? These skills and achievements of your pupils are termed *objectives*. One point to stress though is that an objective should be a measurable outcome or change in the pupils' behaviour rather than a description of what the class will experience. Allied to this is the need to check that your pupils have met the objectives you planned: how are you going to assess this; is there an alternative way for the pupil who finds writing difficult to produce a record of their work? What questions are you going to ask? What are you going to look for during a practical that would prove to both you and your pupils that the relevant skills have been mastered? (Assessment is addressed in Chapter 4 and practical work in Chapter 10.)

Second, your planning will enable you to arrange for the apparatus, other materials and ICT facilities you are likely to need in the lesson. Technicians are busy people, as are those who carry out photocopying of your worksheets, and need advance warning of materials you will need. For example, should you want to demonstrate the structure of a lung, it is unlikely that your school will have one conveniently to hand.

Third, lesson planning allows you to consider the structure of your lesson, especially how long you intend each activity should last. Placing each activity on a timeline allows you to gauge how long your pupils will be sitting inactive and listening to you. An introduction lasting longer than five to ten minutes is likely to result in boredom, inattention and disruptive behaviour.

Fourth, planning enables you to consider the support you provide for the pupils who struggle, those who prefer to learn in a style different to the one you propose (see Chapter 2 for further consideration of learning styles) and the extension activities for those who would benefit from a more demanding challenge. Should you be fortunate enough to have the support of a classroom assistant, how can you direct their activities if you have no clear idea of what it is that you want your pupils to achieve?

Finally, having a suitable record of your lessons avoids you having to start again from scratch the next time you teach the topic. Having resources you have found to work will save you time and effort in the future. Allied to this point is the need to review your lessons; keeping a record of what worked well and what should be changed for the next time will avoid you constantly repeating the same mistakes.

Personal response

Above are some of the reasons for planning lessons carefully in advance. What other factors would you choose to add to the list?

Practical implications and activities

Consider the reasons stated above in favour of planning lessons in advance as well as any additional ones you may wish to add. Try to place the reasons in an order of priority. Consult with a colleague and justify your order of priority to them.

What

As a result of feedback from our own trainees and information gleaned from discussions with mentors, it is clear that the vast majority of schools require their teachers both to have lesson objectives and to explicitly share them with their pupils, although there are still some classrooms where this is not the norm. To this end, it is common to find a separate mini-whiteboard upon which the teacher is expected to display their lesson objectives. Most teachers use the term 'objectives' but some go just that little bit further and display the acronyms WALT (we are learning today), coupled with WILF (what I am looking for), indications of what the teacher expects the pupils to have mastered as well as making it clear how it can be recognised when these skills manifest themselves. This approach goes one step further towards providing pupils with clear guidance as to what they are expected to learn as a result of their lessons since, to use an oft-quoted adage, 'If you don't know where you are going, how will you know when you have got there?' We would make a distinction between these approaches and ones where a title is displayed on the board describing the activities the class are to be engaged in, mistakenly believing this to be an objective. Whilst this approach alerts the pupils to what they will be doing, it does not make clear what changes in their skills or abilities are expected as a result of the lesson and, as such, will be of little use in alerting the pupils as to what they are expected to learn.

Before your read the extract below, read:

- Wellington, J. (2000) Teaching and Learning Secondary Science (pages 47–48). London: Routledge.

Some 50 years ago, Bloom (1956) presented a hierarchy of educational behavioural objectives from the least challenging to the most demanding. In the passage below, he outlines some of his thinking.

Extract: Bloom, B. S. (1956) *Taxonomy of Educational Objectives*. Longman. Pages 1–2.

Most readers will have heard of the biological taxonomies which permit classification into such categories as phyllum, class, order, family, genus, species, variety. Biologists have found their taxonomy markedly helpful as a means of insuring accuracy of communication about their science and as a means of understanding the organization and interrelation of the various parts of the animal and plant world. You are reading about an attempt to build a taxonomy of educational objectives. It is intended to provide for classification of the goals of our educational system. It is expected to be of general help to all teachers, administrators, professional specialists, and research workers who deal with curricular and evaluation problems. It is especially intended to help them discuss these problems, with greater precision. For example, some teachers believe their students should 'really understand,' others desire their students to 'internalize knowledge,' still others want their students to 'grasp the core or essence' or 'comprehend.' Do they all mean the same thing? Specifically, what does a student do who 'really understands' which he does not do when he does not understand? Through reference to the taxonomy as a set of standard classifications, teachers should be able to define such nebulous terms as those given above. This should facilitate the exchange of information about their curricular developments and evaluation devices. Such interchanges are frequently disappointing now because all too frequently what appears to be common ground between schools disappears on closer examination of the descriptive terms being used.

But beyond this, the taxonomy should be a source of constructive help on these problems. Teachers building a curriculum should find here a range of possible educational goals or outcomes in the cognitive area ('cognitive' is used to include activities such as remembering and recalling knowledge, thinking, problem solving, creating). Comparing the goals of their present curriculum with the range of possible outcomes may suggest additional goals they may wish to include. As a further aid, sample objectives chosen from a range of subject-matter fields (though mostly from the upper educational levels) are used to illustrate each of the taxonomy categories. These may be suggestive of the kinds of objectives that could be included in their own curriculum.

Analysis

Bloom's intention was, to a certain extent, one of clarification in that if all in education were using the same terms to represent the same idea it would at least lay the foundations for common language and assist communication. In an attempt to make clear the term being referred to, he defined an objective as:

a statement of how thoughts, feelings and actions of the child will change as a result of the learning experiences provided.

The result of Bloom's work then was a hierarchy of objectives, which he referred to as a 'taxonomy'. The demands of the objectives increase as you move from a lower to a higher level, with a higher-level objective subsuming all lower-level ones. Table 1.1 contains a brief outline of Bloom's taxonomy and, in addition to his own definition of what each level entails, we have added illustrations based upon the process of distillation.

Table 1.1 Bloom's taxonomy, with examples

Level	Objective	Description	Example
1	Knowledge	Simple knowledge of fact	Recall the names of parts of apparatus used in fractional distillation
2	Understanding	Understanding the meaning of the knowledge	Define the role of each part of the apparatus
3	Application	The ability to apply the knowledge to new and concrete situations	Carry out the distillation of ethanol and water
4	Analysis	The ability to break knowledge down into its constituent parts and see the relationship between them	Describe what is happening in each stage of the distillation
5	Synthesis	The ability to reassemble these parts into a new and meaningful relationship	Modify the apparatus to use it to separate another mixture, such as crude oil
6	Evaluation	The ability to judge the value of material using explicit and coherent criteria	Assess the effectiveness of the separation and suggest improvements

Personal response

Consider your own investigations in science. Did you find evaluation to be the most challenging part of your work? What was it about the process that you found challenging?

> ## Practical implications and activities
>
> - Look at the evaluation section of pupils' investigations. Are they as successful in this aspect of their investigational work as the rest? Do your findings support or reject Bloom's suggestion that evaluation is the most challenging of objectives?
> - Choose any topic from either the Key Stage 3 or 4 section of the National Curriculum and construct a hierarchy of objectives for the topic, similar to the example in Table 1.1. Discuss your suggestions with your mentor or a colleague.

One question you might ask is, 'What evidence is there that explicitly sharing objectives with pupils is of benefit?' Objectives have been found to be of benefit on two levels. First, Roopchand and Moss (1988) found that there are significant gains in learning when systematically designed learning materials are employed, which perhaps in some way may be explained by the earlier findings of Roopchand (1987) who, in a similar study, reported greatly improved student behaviour and active learning. In similar studies, Kallinson (1986) reports that the more aware learners are of the objectives and reasons for the structure of a lesson, the higher their retention rate of material being studied. Lewis (1984) supports the usefulness of objectives since:

> They help the learner to plan his work and to take on responsibility for his own learning, and to help him check progress towards achieving the aims of the course.

This thinking resonates with the earlier work of Ausubel (1960), who defined 'advance organisers' as the devices used in the introduction of a topic which enable learners to orient themselves to the topic, so that they can locate where any particular bit of input fits in and how it links with what they already know.

How

Planning within school will probably occur on three different levels: long, medium and short term. Long-term planning is likely to cover a period of several months, even up to years in advance, and a department would outline how the teaching is to be broken down into a series of units to provide continuity and progression. The shorter, more detailed units, covering perhaps a single topic, lasting for a few weeks, are termed *schemes of work*. As a trainee teacher your school placement you should be provided with a scheme of work to serve as a guide from which to prepare individual lesson plans. You would not be expected to write schemes of work during your placement. However, a valuable opportunity may arise during a school placement to prepare a scheme of work alongside an experienced teacher and in the extract below, Parkinson (1994) outlines what he believes should be provided in a scheme of work document.

Before you read the extract, read:

- Wellington, J. (2000) *Teaching and Learning Secondary Science* (pages 109–110). London: Routledge.

Extract: Parkinson, J. (1994) *The Effective Teaching of Secondary Science*. Longman. Pages 75–78.

The terms 'scheme of work (SoW)', 'learning programme' and 'teaching scheme' are different ways of saying the same thing. A scheme of work sets out the teaching sequence for a topic together with other key details such as resources, assessment opportunities and outline practical details together with their risk assessment. The starting point for the development of a SoW will be a syllabus or the PoS of the NC science document. It should take into account the school's policy on curriculum and assessment. It will generally be the job of the head of department or the head of a key stage to prepare the SoW. Trainee teachers will find it useful to talk to staff involved with preparing the document and in examining the logic behind the sequence of lessons. The scheme will probably be built up by an examination of the syllabus, a series of appropriate textbooks and the assessment requirements of the course. Teachers frequently work together in planning the SoW, considering such things as the most appropriate sequence of lessons, the inclusion of practical activities and the quantity of learning activity that can be accomplished in any one lesson.

As a trainee teacher you should find the SoW to be a very useful document to work from as it contains a lot of information in a compact form. At a glance you can see the sequence of lessons and check that the pupils are receiving a variety of learning activities. It will give you an overall picture of the assessment opportunities thus helping you to plan ahead. When you have completed the teaching of the topic you can again turn to the SoW and use it as a first step in reviewing the effectiveness of your work. Headteachers and inspectors also find these schemes useful as it enables them to see at a glance how the NC is being implemented in science.

Content of a SoW

Not unnaturally you will find that different teachers interpret the production of a SoW in different ways. On the most simplistic level you will have a list of topics in the order that they are to be taught. The more sophisticated the SoW, the longer it takes to prepare. It can be very disheartening for teachers who have prepared very thorough SoWs only to find that the syllabus is about to change the following year. As we seem to be living in an era of constant curriculum change it is advisable to prepare the scheme on a word processor so that it can be easily revised.

HMI have suggested that a good SoW should:

- specify the skills, ideas and attitudes that are expected to arise as a result of the science teaching in the course
- give details of what is to be taught, and the order in which it is to be tackled
- suggest ways of teaching the material, related to the aims and objectives of the course
- give notes on the apparatus available
- indicate the depth of treatment required

In addition you should include cross-references to the syllabus or NC and information about safety or a risk assessment reference. Guidance for the production of SoWs can be found in publications from the ASE and the non-statutory guidance for NC science. Just as with the preparation of lesson plans, there is no one set method but you may find the following guide useful.

A SoW should include the information below.

1. A sequenced and approximately timed set of lessons. In constructing this you will need to take into account:
- The degree of difficulty of the science concepts involved.
- What previous knowledge are the pupils likely to bring to these lessons?
- How can the work be sequenced so that each lesson builds on the work learned in the previous lessons?

2. A list of appropriate teaching activities.
- What are the learning objectives and what teaching strategies do I need to adopt in order to achieve those objectives? This will help to determine the time allocation required in (1).
- Practical activities must refer to a risk assessment.

3. Guidance regarding differentiation within each learning activity. This should include indications of:

- Strategies for managing learning in mixed-ability classes.
- Learning difficulties that many pupils experience with particular topics.
- Suggestions for extension work.

4. Assessment opportunities. This should include:

- Cross-referencing to the SoAs of the National Curriculum or other science syllabus.
- Methods of assessment.
- Criteria for assessment, i.e. transposing the SoAs to the particular situation being studied during the lesson.

5. Suggestions for homework.

6. Resources required. This should include:

- Textbooks to be used with the page references.
- Other written materials, e.g. worksheets, pamphlets, posters (reference to the location of these documents).
- Apparatus and equipment including audiovisual (reference to the company supplying the video etc.).

Analysis

As Parkinson indicates, there are advantages to groups of teachers sharing the responsibility of writing a scheme of work, namely that:

- the workload is shared;
- the approach to the teaching is likely to be common, giving equality of opportunity for the groups;
- it acts as a learning opportunity for less experienced practitioners.

It is doubtful that a trainee teacher would be able to teach directly from a scheme of work but it should serve as a valuable tool to monitor, for example, that a range of activities suited to different preferred learning styles (see Chapter 2) has been considered. In addition, it should give advance warning to the technical staff of experiments that require setting up well in advance or of apparatus to be purchased.

Personal response

In addition to the advantages noted above, consider other benefits to be gained from preparing detailed schemes of work.

Planning an individual lesson is the next stage in the process, an activity that trainee teachers find time-consuming and difficult at the start while experienced teachers seem to give the impression that it is a simple, straightforward activity. For an experienced teacher, a brief note in a planner for each lesson would probably serve to remind them of what is intended. It is not, as noted earlier, that the experienced teachers fail to plan but that the planning has become internalised over the years. For the beginning teacher, though, it is a different matter, as everything is new, and once immersed in the lesson it is easy to forget what was intended, so a detailed prompt is of great value.

Returning once again to the issue of objectives: your pupils are not the only ones to be learning from your lesson. You are a learner as well and it is helpful for your own progress to make a note of a skill that you would aim to improve as a result of the lesson. Setting and reviewing your own personal objectives is a valuable tool in your personal development. (For a more detailed consideration of self-development, see Blandford, 2003.)

Having composed your learning objectives for the lesson, you next need to consider the activities best suited to their attainment and matched to the characteristics of your class, bearing in mind such issues as safety, inclusion and differentiation. But, having selected the most appropriate activity, how are you going to gain the class's interest? How are you going to make the material relevant? What is the context? The average 14-year-old is unlikely to want to know about the Haber Process unless they can see a use or link to their everyday life. A short starter activity to engage the pupils and focus their attention is required. At some point during the lesson or at the end, whichever is the most appropriate time, you will also have to consider how you are going to test to see if the pupils' learning objectives have been met. This might be via a question-and-answer session, a pupil presentation, worksheet completion, a test, some form of a game or any other suitable process. The common description for this activity is a *plenary session* and it can be both fun and productive to involve your pupils in creating suitable questions to check that learning has taken place, rather than you imposing yours upon them.

Practical implications and activities

- Consider a recent lesson that you have either taught or observed.
- Plan an activity that you could have used to start the lesson that lasted no longer than five minutes that is relevant to the material being covered and would have engaged the class. Discuss your idea with your mentor.
- Inspect the lesson plan provided and make a note of any additional aspects you would wish to add for your own personal use. Are there any major omissions that you think should have been included? Discuss your suggestions with a colleague or your mentor.
- Devise a game-like activity that you could use in a plenary session.

Further reading

Blandford, S. (2003) *Professional Development Manual*. London: Pearson.

Bloom, B. S. (1956) *Taxonomy of Educational Objectives. Handbook 1: The Cognitive Domain*. London: Longmans Green.

DfES (2004) *Pedagogy and Practice: Teaching and Learning in Secondary Schools. Unit 1: Structuring learning*. Norwich: HMSO.

Joyce, B., Calhoun, E. and Hopkins, D. (2002) *Models of Learning: Tools for Teaching*. Buckingham: Open University Press.

Parker, J. (2004) *Badger Key Stage 3 Science Starters* (Y7/Y8/Y9). Stevenage: Badger Publishing.

2 Addressing pupils' learning styles

By the end of this chapter you will have considered and reflected upon:

- **what** is understood by learning styles;
- **why** pupils' preferred learning styles need to be considered when planning lessons;
- **how** strategies may be developed that cater for pupils with a range of learning styles.

Linking your learning
Achieving QTS Reflective Reader: Secondary Professional Studies. Hoult, S. (2005) Chapter 3.

Professional Standards for QTS
2.1c, 2.4, 2.7, 3.1.2, 3.3.1, 3.3.2c, 3.3.3

Introduction

It can be extremely frustrating for a teacher to have prepared an interesting and challenging lesson, only to find that a section of the class not only fails to engage with the material but becomes disruptive and disturbs those who want to learn. When discussing the issue in the staffroom, the frustration is compounded when a teacher in another subject area reports that the same pupils not only behave well for them but that they engage with the material and are making good progress. This scenario is not uncommon and can lead to teachers doubting their abilities and animosity between them and their pupils. Is it a case of the subject matter being beyond the capabilities of the pupils, a poor teacher, unreceptive pupils or a mismatch between the way the material is being presented and the way in which the pupils prefer to learn?

What

In order for information to enter the long-term memory store of an individual, it is thought to pass through several information-processing components (Riding, 2002) and a schematic view of this process is shown below:

| Information to be learned | → | The senses – for example, seeing and hearing | → | Working memory | → ← | Cognitive style | → ← | Long-term memory |

Information is received by the senses, for example in the form of pictures and written words to the eyes and sounds and speech to the ears. This information is then transferred to the working memory, which can be considered to be a temporary store which can hold a limited amount of information (about seven items) for a short while (only seconds) while we work out the meaning of what we see and hear before passing it (or not) on to the long-term memory, where the information is linked to what we already know.

The *cognitive style* of an individual is their preferred and habitual approach to organising and representing information when passing it on to the long-term memory. Although a person's cognitive style may be considered immutable, the processes used by the learner to mediate between the cognitive style and incoming data are slightly more flexible and it is probably more appropriate to refer to this as an individual's preferred learning style. Riding (2002) suggests that a person's cognitive style could be represented by two dimensions.

- Does the individual take a whole view (wholist) or see things in parts (analytic)?
- Is the individual outgoing and verbal (verbaliser) or inward-looking, often thinking in mental pictures or images (imager)?

Information is thought to be stored in an individual's long-term memory in two forms (Paivio, 1900), namely in a linguistic and a visual form.

However, Riding's views are not the only ones to have been put forward with relevance to teaching and learning. Although strictly not related to learning styles but still of importance to the teacher's understanding of how pupils learn is intelligence. Howard Gardner (1984) proposed that individuals do not possess a single global intelligence but a range of intelligences. These are:

- logical-mathematical intelligence – the capacity to handle mathematical patterns and long-chain reasoning;
- linguistic intelligence – the capacity to use written and oral language;
- spatial intelligence – the capacity to perceive the visual spatial world and transform perceptions spatially;
- bodily-kinaesthetic intelligence – the capacity to control one's bodily movements and to handle objects skilfully;
- musical intelligence – the capacity to produce and appreciate music;
- interpersonal intelligence – the capacity to be aware of and sensitive to the emotions of others;
- intrapersonal intelligence – the ability to understand one's own knowledge strengths, weaknesses, desires and intelligence.

Personal response

- Refer to Riding's two dimensions of cognitive style and consider where you might place yourself on the two dimensions.
- Refer to Gardner's original seven intelligences and consider which combination or individual intelligence best describes yourself.

Practical implications and activities

Consult a scheme of work that you have just taught from and, in the light of Gardner's seven intelligences, annotate the scheme to indicate which sections address which intelligence(s). Are there any intelligences that are not addressed and how might you amend the scheme of work to include all seven?

Before you read the extract, read:

- Hoult, S. (2005) *Achieving QTS: Reflective Reader Secondary Professional Studies* (page 45) Exeter: Learning Matters.

Extract: White, J. (2000) *Do Howard Gardner's Multiple Intelligences Add Up?* Institute of Education. Pages 1–3.

How many of your intelligences have you used today?

An odd question? Not to the students in an Australian school who pass this message on a board each day on their way out of the building. For their schooling is based, like that of a rapidly growing number of pupils in the USA, Britain and elsewhere, on the theory of Multiple Intelligences (MI) produced by the Harvard psychologist Howard Gardner.

Howard Gardner published his book *Frames of Mind* in 1983. In it he argued for the existence of a small number of relatively discrete 'intelligences' in human beings, combinable in different ways to form the intellectual repertoire of different individuals. Two of these, logico-mathematical intelligence and linguistic intelligence, are what IQ tests have focused on. But intelligence is more multiplex than this: other intelligences include the musical, the spatial, the bodily-kinaesthetic, the intrapersonal and the interpersonal. His recent research has added to the original seven both the classificatory intelligence of the naturalist and – he has some doubts on this one – spiritual intelligence. He says, half seriously, that while Socrates viewed human beings as rational animals, he himself sees them as animals possessing eight-and-a-half intelligences (Craft, 1997:6).

The impact of MI theory on school reform

A discussion in 1998 of a 15-year-old theory may appear belated. I engage in it only because Gardner's views about multiple intelligences have grown increasingly influential over the years. He is now one of the best known experts on intelligence not only in America but across the world, and a leading contributor to the debates on Herrnstein's and Murray's *The Bell Curve* (1994). In addition, thousands of so-called 'MI schools' have sprung up in recent years in America, Canada, Australia and elsewhere, all based on his theory. Some of Gardner's disciples, as in the Australian example with which we began, believe that the curriculum should be based on the development of all the 'intelligences'. Gardner himself (1993:71) sees more educational mileage in recognizing that pupils 'have quite different minds from each other', and that 'education should be so sculpted that it remains responsive to these differences'.

His ideas are also currently influential in Britain. His notion of multiple intelligences is widely referred to by those involved in school reform, both at school and local authority level, and in educational research. In particular, MI theory has recently become a liberating force in school improvement projects across the country, from Sandwell and Birmingham in the West Midlands to Govan in Scotland. It is not difficult to see why such a notion should appeal to teachers and policy-makers working in deprived areas and faced with underachievement. Many children in these areas are held back by a low self-concept. They see themselves as dim or thick. But this is within the framework of the traditional version of intelligence – they are poor at the kind of abstract logical thinking that IQ tests target. Broaden the picture and their perceptions are transformed. 'Children are born smart', as a project leader from Birmingham puts it. Their abilities may lie in physical activities, in music, in the visual arts, in interactions with other people. Extended learning schemes in West Midland, Glasgow and other schools tap into these and other areas. Once children become aware of how intelligent they are in this field or that, their self-esteem is said to increase amazingly. A project worker from Sandwell put it to Howard Gardner like this: 'The strength we get from your work is that you do use the word "intelligence", because the kids have been told so often – not explicitly, but they have picked up the message that they are not intelligent, that they don't have this chunk of intelligence' (Craft, 1997:19).

Analysis

The idea that intelligence is not restricted to the abilities that would enable an individual to score highly in an IQ test would certainly have appeal in an educational world where teachers are endeavouring to convince their pupils that they are not lacking in intelligence. The motivational effects of espousing the idea of multiple intelligences, one could claim, might encourage the adoption of a mantra in which each child has its own intelligence, only the formal tests used to assess it are somehow flawed and fail to recognise the fact.

Taking a critical stance with respect to Gardner's multiple intelligences, White (1998) describes his theory as 'decidedly flaky' and questions the intelligences selected, asserting that:

> Gardner's examples of high levels of development in the intelligences seem to reflect his own value judgements about what kinds of qualities are important.

White further asserts that Gardner's intelligences show a heavy bias towards aesthetic considerations, with only two of the original seven (logico-mathematical and interpersonal) not having an artistic flavour to them. In a quest for an algorithm for Gardner's selection of an intelligence to add to the list, White cites Gardner's own words that:

> It must be admitted that the selection (or rejection) of a candidate intelligence is reminiscent more of an artistic judgement than of a scientific assessment.

An admission, perhaps, by Gardner that the identification of intelligence is a subjective matter? If this is the case, could it not be that a viable alternative list of intelligences might be constructed?

Why

For the teacher, there are several important issues arising from the models outlined in the section above.

First, if the information to be stored is such that the individual can form links between new and existing data, then long-term storage is less challenging. For example, referring to a Persian cat is likely to be relatively easy for a pupil if they can relate to existing images of cats. Conversely, referring to a quagga would probably not be as easy since the concept may be alien to most pupils. However, if the pupils were told that the quagga is a now-extinct animal, similar to a zebra and a horse, once thought to inhabit Africa, then the idea is likely to be less challenging to assimilate.

Since the working memory of most humans is relatively small (Miller, 1956) and can only hold a limited amount of information for a few seconds, it would be wise to restrict the number of ideas presented to children at any one time since any new information entering this working space is replacing existing, decaying ideas. For example, if you ask a pupil to fetch a Bunsen, a beaker, a thermometer, a length of rubber tube and a clamp stand, it would be unwise to start adding additional pieces of equipment to the list as they walk away since you are probably likely to get the newer items but not all of the original ones. When weak readers are faced with over-long sentences, by the time they get to the end of the sentence it is likely that they may have forgotten the beginning and the whole sentence becomes unintelligible.

Similarly, if a pupil has a hard-wired system of organising and representing material before it is passed on to the long-term memory store, it would be unproductive for that individual to have information presented to him or her in a manner that did not sit comfortably with their own preferred style of information processing.

The message from Gardner's work is that in our teaching we should seek to draw upon the strengths that individuals possessing different intelligences may have. However, careful thought should be given to the activities employed; since running around does not in its self exercise bodily/kinaesthetic intelligence, neither is simply having music playing in the background likely to do anything to enhance the performance of pupils strong in musical intelligence; Gardner (1995) describes such use of multiple intelligences as 'trivial'. Effective use of musical intelligence would need to get the pupils thinking musically or drawing upon the structural aspects of music in order to illuminate the concepts in other fields such as maths.

There is evidence to suggest that when pupils use both visual and linguistic processing powers, information is both understood and recalled better (DfES, 2004). Additional works indicate that activities which enhance the creation of non-linguistic representations in the mind include:

- drawing pictures (Newton, 1995);
- generating mental images (Willoughby et al., 1997);
- constructing physical models (Welch, 1997);
- engaging in kinaesthetic activities (Aubusson et al., 1997).

On the basis of this evidence, it would therefore seem prudent to present learners with activities which include a combination of visual, auditory and kinaesthetic (VAK) experiences.

The statutory inclusion statement in the science National Curriculum (DfES/QCA, 2004, pp. 40–48) places a responsibility upon teachers to provide effective learning opportunities for all pupils and, in order to do so, teachers are required to:

- plan their approaches to teaching and learning so that all pupils can take part in lessons fully and effectively;
- secure motivation and concentration by using teaching approaches appropriate to different learning styles;
- use appropriate assessment approaches that allow for different learning styles and ensure that pupils are given the chance and encouragement to demonstrate their competence and attainment through appropriate means.

In their advice on how to cater for differing learning styles in the classroom, the DfES (2004) state that there is often a mismatch between the preferred learning styles of pupils and the learning opportunities presented to them. Reasons for this mismatch are given as:

- a lack of understanding of the range of learning styles within the class;
- the impossibility of addressing the full range of preferred learning styles within any one classroom;
- the tendency of teachers to teach according to their own preferred learning style;
- an unwillingness to provide a range of outcomes because some may be difficult to assess;
- the likelihood of pupils making inappropriate choices from a range of tasks, which perpetuates the mismatch;
- a concern for behaviour management when using kinaesthetic activities;
- time constraints in producing materials.

How

In order to cater for the varied learning styles in any given class, it would be of use to identify the way individuals prefer to learn. It is possible to locate interactive tests on the Internet and have pupils complete them, there being some merit to this strategy, although caution should be exercised when using such tests, which are often aimed at an adult, rather than younger audience. An alternative approach is to observe and talk to individuals, using your observations to give an indication of their preferred learning style. Talking to individuals about their favourite learning activities and subjects can help build this profile. Table 2.1 contains guidelines which may prove helpful in deciding whether an individual is a visual, auditory or kinaesthetic learner.

Table 2.1 Traits of different learning styles

Visual	Auditory	Kinaesthetic
Prefers to read, see the words, illustrations and diagrams	Likes to be told, to listen to the teacher, to talk it out	Likes to get involved, hands-on, to try it out
Talks fast, uses lots of images	Talks fluently, in a logical order and with few hesitations	Talks about actions and feelings, uses lots of hand movements, speaks more slowly
Memorises by writing repeatedly	Memorises by repeating words out loud	Memorises by doing something repeatedly
When inactive, looks around, doodles or watches something	When inactive, talks to self or others	When inactive, fidgets and walks around
When starts to understand something says, 'that looks right'	When starts to understand something says, 'that sounds right'	When starting to understand something says, 'that feels right'
Is most distracted by untidiness	Is most distracted by noises	Is most distracted by movements or physical disturbances

(Adapted from DfES, 2004)

Having identified pupils' preferred learning styles, although preferable, it would be unrealistic to plan every single lesson to take into account the learning styles of each individual. This is not an issue as long as, over a period of time (say a particular topic or module) a range of differing preferred learning styles is catered for and individuals are not ignored; no individual preferred learning style should be omitted for three lessons in a row, otherwise there is a danger that some pupils will become disengaged.

Guidelines (DfES, 2004) that would allow for differing learning styles and intelligences in your planning include:

- provide a choice of activities so that pupils can opt to used their preferred learning style;
- allow for a range of outcomes in units of work that would allow for differing intelligences (see Gardner's multiple intelligences above);
- avoid teaching to your own preferred style of learning; planning in teams where the members have differing learning styles can help avoid this;
- plan a multi-sensory starter activity if at all possible so that a range of learners are engaged;
- do not allow pupils to work exclusively within their preferred style of learning; encourage them to become more flexible learners.

A summary of experiences and assessment devices that might cater for differing learning styles and intelligences is given in Table 2.2.

Table 2.2 Suggested activities to cater for different learning styles and intelligences

Visual, auditory, kinaesthetic	Multiple intelligence	Learning experience
Visual	Visual-spatial	Diagrams, charts, video, films, graphs, posters, maps, pamphlets, textbooks, drawing, creating mental pictures, collages, colour highlighting
Auditory	Linguistic	Discussion, group work, pair work, debates, interviewing, expositions, presentations, improvisations, listening to speakers, mnemonics, writing notes, essays and poems, sketches stories, reading
Kinaesthetic	Bodily- kinaesthetic	DARTs, role play, dance, model making, simulations, 'show me' cards, freeze-frames, improvisation, associating ideas with movements, human graphs, sentences or timelines, field trips, games, competitions
	Logical-mathematical	Puzzles, problem-solving, predicting or hypothesising, investigations, sequential tasks, summaries, pattern spotting
	Musical	Chants, rhymes, songs, mnemonics, raps, poems, musical interpretations
	Interpersonal	Collaborative group, pair or team work, interviewing, teaching or coaching others
	Intrapersonal	Individual research, learning journals, reflection on own learning, identifying own questions, self-evaluation, diaries

(Adapted from DfES, 2003 Teaching and Learning in Secondary Schools: Unit 10: Learning Styles. London: DfES)

Personal response

Consult Table 2.1 and consider which learning style you favour yourself. Bear this in mind when planning activities for your classes.

Practical implications and activities

- In consultation with your mentor, select a group of pupils in any one class who are considered to be underachieving and, using the traits in Table 2.1, decide which preferred learning style each of them is likely to favour.
- Examine the most recent scheme of work that has been used to construct lessons for the class and, using Table 2.2, analyse it to see if any learning style is used more frequently than another. Is one learning style being neglected?

- Compare the likely learning styles for your group of underachieving pupils with those being used and consider if there is a mismatch between the two.
- If there is a mismatch, how might the scheme of work be modified to present a more equitable learning experience for pupils?

Further reading

Blandford, S. (2005) *Sonia Blandford's Masterclass*. London: Sage.

Dickinson, C. (1996) *Effective Learning Activities*. Stafford: Network Educational Press.

DfES (2003) *Pedagogy and Practice: Teaching and Learning in Secondary Schools. Unit 19: Learning Styles*. Norwich: HMSO.

Gardner, H. (1983) *Frames of Mind*. London: Heinemann.

Gardner, H. (1995) Reflections on Multiple Intelligences: myths and messages, *Phi-Delta Kappa*, 77 (3), 200–209.

Riding, R. (2002) *School Learning and Cognitive Style*. London: David Fulton.

Riding, R. and Rayner, S. (2005) *Cognitive Styles and Learning Strategies*. London: David Fulton.

3 Inclusion and special needs in science

By the end of this chapter you should have considered and reflected upon:

- **what** is understood by inclusion and special needs in the secondary school curriculum;
- **why** inclusion and special needs should be considered when developing learning and teaching strategies for science in secondary schools;
- **how** learning and teaching episodes, in science, can be developed which address inclusion and special needs.

Linking your learning
Achieving QTS Reflective Reader: Secondary Professional Studies. Hoult, S. (2005) Chapter 7.
Achieving QTS Reflective Reader: Primary Special Educational Needs. Soan, S. (2005) Chapter 4.

Professional Standards for QTS
1.2, 1.3, 1.6, 3.1.2, 3.1.3, 3.3.3, 3.3.4, 3.3.7, 3.3.9

Introduction

It is often assumed by beginning teachers that the terms 'inclusion', 'special needs' and, to some extent, 'differentiation' are either mutually exclusive issues or ones which require radically different solutions (Gibson and Blandford, 2005). As with most issues in learning and teaching, solutions depend on planning. If you have not already done so, study Chapter 1, 'Planning for effective learning in science', where detailed advice on planning can be found.

In this chapter you will be reflecting on inclusion, special needs and differentiation in science and how they may be addressed.

To help schools consider inclusive education a non-statutory code of practice (DfES, 2001) exists which schools are required to have regard for in their policy documents and practice.

What

Inclusion is generally accepted, as needing an active response from the educational setting.

> *In our view, inclusion is a set of never-ending processes. It involves the specification of the direction of change. It is relevant to any school however inclusive or exclusive its current cultures, policies and practices.*

> (Booth et al., 2000)

So, if inclusion requires an active response from the setting, can we assume that the absence of such a response is implicit in the opposite, exclusion? In looking at the evidence on exclusions it is the case that some groups are excluded disproportionately when compared to others:

- four times as many boys than girls are excluded;
- black pupils experience six times the rate of exclusion of white pupils;
- children with statements of special educational needs experience exclusion six times more than their proportion in the school population;
- travellers, young carers, pregnant schoolgirls and teenage mothers are known to be vulnerable to exclusion.

(Adapted from Hayden and Dunne, 2001)

Inclusion is a complex issue, of that there is no doubt, but the DfES (2001) in the revised Code of Practice for Special Educational Needs stresses inclusive education and inclusive practices as its main aim. However, this is not the first time inclusive education has received such support since both UNESCO (1994) and the UK Human Rights Act (1998) both argue that the notion of inclusion and participation in education are essential to human dignity:

> *The fundamental principle of the inclusive school is that all children should learn together, wherever possible … Inclusive schooling is the most effective means for building solidarity between children with special needs and their peers.*
> (UNESCO, 1994)

This being the case, what stands in the way of inclusive practice, since it is obviously not common to all schools? We will briefly consider three: local politicians, teachers and parents. Starting with local government, via the local education authority (LEA), the DfEE (2000) defined their responsibilities as: special educational needs, school transport, school improvement, education of excluded pupils, pupil welfare and strategic management. By giving the responsibility of inclusion to the LEA this now makes provision variable across, and within, LEAs. Ainscow (1999) writes that within LEAs officials often have their own contradictory definitions of inclusion and some LEAs 'pretend to adopt' government policy whilst acting in what they consider to be the best local action. Thus although the DfES (2002) publication *The Distribution of Resources to Support Inclusion* provides LEAs with exemplars of best practice, if they choose to ignore this then no enforcement mechanism exists.

Imagine what it must be like for a parent. All parents want what is best for their child but, not surprisingly, they want the best 'social environment, the best academic environment, the best personal environment, the best cultural environment and the best physical environment. There are bound to be contradictions' (Nind and Sheehy, 2004). In addition, much like other issues, e.g. HIV, BSE and MMR, parents are swamped by 'expert' advice from all possible media outlets.

Surely teachers must be central to any programme of inclusive education. Unfortunately, the research into teacher attitudes is also conflicting. A review of 28 research studies into teacher attitudes, covering some 37 years, revealed that whilst two-thirds of teachers supported the notion of inclusion, less than half saw it as a realistic option and only one-third believed that a mainstream school was the best setting and even less believing they had the resources, skills or training to implement inclusive practice (Scruggs and Mastropieri, 1996).

So, to conclude this section, what should inclusive education involve? Booth and Ainscow (2002) suggest the following:

- Valuing all students and staff equally.
- Increasing the participation of students in, and reducing their exclusion from, the cultures, curricula and communities of local schools.
- Restructuring the cultures, policies and practices in schools so that they respond to the diversity of students in the locality.
- Reducing barriers to learning and participation for all students, not only those with impairments or those who are categorised as 'having special educational needs'.
- Learning from attempts to overcome barriers to the access and participation of particular students to make changes for the benefit of students more widely.
- Viewing the difference between students as resources to support learning, rather than as problems to be overcome.
- Acknowledging the right of students to an education in their locality.
- Improving schools for staff as well as for students.
- Emphasising the role of schools in building community and developing values, as well as in increasing achievement.
- Fostering mutually sustaining relationships between schools and communities.
- Recognising that inclusion in education is one aspect of inclusion in society.

Personal response

Think of a time when, as a learner of science either at school, college or university, you simply didn't get it when all the others did. Did you still feel part of the group? What strategies did your peers and teacher(s) employ to 'include' you?

Practical implications and activities

Discuss with your school-based mentor your definition of inclusion. How closely does it match that of your mentor and that given in the school's policy?
Plan a lesson and discuss with both your mentor and the school's SENCO how they view it in terms of inclusivity.
Deliver the planned lesson and have your mentor observe. After the lesson revisit your definition of inclusion. What changes, if any, would you make?

Why

Having considered what is to be understood by the term 'inclusion', we will now consider why inclusion is important in planning for effective science teaching.
One could simply take a legal stance by referring to the 1988 Education Reform Act, which sets out clearly that all pupils are entitled to receive a broad and balanced education in the National Curriculum and that the teaching they receive addresses their

needs. This is not simply a case of catering for those with learning issues but also catering for behavioural, emotional and physical issues that a pupil may present with. In addition, since these are most often overlooked, the 'gifted and talented' pupil has a unique set of special needs and issues for inclusion in the lesson.

We could also argue from the standards trainee teachers are required to demonstrate, as set out in *Qualifying to Teach,* in order to achieve qualified teacher status (QTS):

- 1.1 You have high expectations of all pupils; respect their social, cultural, linguistic, religious and ethnic backgrounds; and are committed to raising their educational achievement
- 3.3.1 You have high expectations of pupils and build successful relationships, centred on teaching and learning. You establish a purposeful learning environment where diversity is valued and where pupils feel secure and confident.

(DfEE, 2002)

Rather than take the legal argument we would like you, the reader, to consider why science educators should take time to plan for inclusion and special needs.

Ross et al. (2000) suggest that science education 'by its nature, includes a whole range of characteristics' which proffer unique benefits, including:

- a practical approach, nurturing first-hand experiences;
- potential for group or collaborative work and peer support;
- conceptual development in sequential steps affording opportunities for success;
- development of understanding of the 'big ideas' in science – those broad conceptual areas which allow for internal differentiation and individual progression.

Drawing on your own experience as a learner and your time on placement in school, you are advised to consider the above and reflect on the occasions when you have seen any of the unique benefits in action.

Nicholls and Turner (1988) suggest perceived benefits of science education for pupils with learning difficulties, which include:

- the importance of first-hand experience;
- the links between science and everyday experiences;
- activities and phenomena that capture the imagination of pupils, enhancing motivation.

It can be seen from the above that science can impact on pupils via increased motivation and the development of social skills. In addition, these benefits contribute to the whole school and wider community by giving value to the notion of inclusion and by helping pupils avoid exclusion.

Personal response

We all want to be included. Think of a time when, perhaps as part of a sports team, you were excluded. What impact did this have on both your motivation and behaviour?

Practical implications and activities

Consider the list of unique benefits of science education given above. With one of your peers or your school-based mentor develop your own list of benefits. How do the two lists compare? How does the uniqueness of science education benefit the pupil, the teacher and society?

How

If we accept that inclusive education is desirable and that school science can make a meaningful contribution to it, how can this be achieved? We offer the following aspects which we consider important for the process of moving from policy to practice in inclusion and special needs education:

- Leadership, in terms of senior leadership commitment to inclusion and training of staff (Gibson and Blandford, 2005).
- Access, in terms of physical and environmental barriers as well as access to the curriculum and learning.
- Differentiation of work and support given. To facilitate access and include all pupils the work set has to appropriate to individual needs, i.e. make the work fit the pupil and not vice versa.
- Equality of practice, local children included in local provision.
- Active participation of pupils, parents, the local community and other professionals.

Of the above, possibly one which trainee or newly qualified teachers feel most able to have an impact on is differentiation. We consider differentiation to be a vital component of inclusive education in science and a first steps towards providing for those with special needs. Remember that it could be argued that all pupils have some special need at some point in their school career.

Before reading the extract below, read:

- Peterson et al. (2000) in Sears, J. and Sorenson, P. (eds.) *Issues in Science Teachings* (pages 196–208). London: Routledge.

Extract: Ross, K., Larkin, L. and Callaghan, P. (2000) *Teaching Secondary Science*. David Fulton Publishers. Pages 159–160.

Good practice for all
The National Curriculum Council Circular N.5 (NCC 1989) stated that good practice in relation to special educational needs is good practice for all. The keystone to this good practice, and indeed the effective learning that accompanies it, is 'differentiation', the process by which activities are matched to the competencies and context of the pupil. Associated with this is effective assessment, used to diagnose areas of difficulty. Activities need to be devised to overcome them and an interactive record of achievement, based on social and personal achievements, developed.

Special needs can best be met when a general concern for individual differences is uppermost in the teachers' thinking. This is all very well, but how can this be achieved with 9T, a mixed-ability, 'middle of the road' science set?

Effective differentiation
Differentiation is achieved by identifying the needs of individuals and developing opportunities to guide, encourage and support learning through whatever resources, processes and tactics are available. For this to be effective, the teacher must get to know the pupils as well as the knowledge, experiences and abilities they bring with them to their lessons. Good record-keeping, and regular marking of pupils' work, achieve this. Armed with this information, discerning teachers can fulfil their role of encouraging independent learning. This learning-centred approach follows the constructivist view of teaching and learning, building on or challenging the pupils' everyday experiences and conceptual models of understanding that develop from them. This follows intervention by the teacher that takes account of the range of ideas from the class. There can be a shift of emphasis from whole-class to individual-based learning, as pupils are encouraged to challenge and discuss their own models against the models presented by the teacher.

Once we know the range of ideas and capabilities of the pupils in our class it is the effective use of differentiation that will ensure that all pupils are working at their best and on the most appropriate activity for them. Following interventions by the teacher a number of differentiation strategies can be used:

Differentiation by task
Differentiated tasks, on a common theme, pitched at various levels of ability, are available around the room, with the pupils being directed to the relevant ones. This approach ensures that the pupils are working within their means.

Differentiation by outcome
Here the task will be the same, but we expect different pupils to achieve differently. Such tasks will have to be 'open-ended' such as creative writing or experimental design, some completing it fairly superficially, while others make a great deal of it.

Differentiation by support
If all the pupils have the same task, and are expected to complete the activity by the end of the lesson, some will need more support from the teacher than others. While we cannot spend all our classroom time helping a minority of pupils, this approach is effective and the more able (or willing) pupils are happy to be given the independence and responsibility to get on by themselves.

Such support can lead to adjustments that make the task or the outcome different. Pupils' responses will provide important information about the suitability of the task, allowing us to adjust the task at that point, making it more challenging for some, and more accessible to others.

Naylor and Keogh (1998) suggest a full range of activities that can be employed to differentiate appropriately and which include the following:

- adjust the level or scientific skills used;
- introduce a range of learning styles such as using structured work cards, designing an

investigation to explore pupils' own ideas, using a computer simulation or textbook for research;

- provide a range of suitable resources;
- adjust the levels of oral/written skills required;
- adjust the levels of mathematical skills required;
- vary the amount and nature of teacher and assistant support;
- vary the degree of pupil independence – investigations serve as a good vehicle for this;
- use suitable questions, prepared in advance;
- vary the response required;
- vary the pace and sequence of the lesson; vary the method of recording and presentation.

These strategies could be employed at any stage in the lesson, as well as being incorporated in your planning. Mention needs to be made here of your use of support staff: always ensure that they are involved in your planning and the production of any worksheets. However, in order to determine the effectiveness of your efforts, ongoing assessment needs to be carried out.

Analysis

The authors start out by making the point that good practice in terms of special needs is good practice for all. Since it can be argued that all pupils, at some time, have some degree of special needs then what they are suggesting is just 'good teaching'.

Moving on to the issue of differentiation, it is made clear in the extract that this is based on knowledge of the pupils and the ability to construct learning and teaching episodes which challenge and support individuals. Returning to the earlier parts of this chapter, we would argue that this is leading us towards an inclusive classroom.

The extract suggests three differentiation strategies: task, outcome and support, each of which can have benefits in a given situation. However, we would argue that differentiation alone is not sufficient for inclusion. Differentiation may allow the teacher to integrate a pupil into the class but unless the teacher, department or school take a proactive role in engaging with the pupil then integration will not develop into inclusion. Inclusion implies a change in the curriculum, assessment, pedagogy and grouping of pupils (Mittler, 2000).

However, the strategies suggested in the extract give the trainee or beginning teacher a template with which to develop their own approach to the inclusive classroom.

Personal response

Consider your own learning at school or university, which differentiation strategies can you recall?

Practical implications and activities

Table 3.1 gives a number of statements regarding differentiation strategies. With a colleague or a mentor, place the statements in order of effectiveness and justify your rank order in terms of the contribution made towards developing an inclusive classroom.

Table 3.1 Differentiation and the inclusive classroom

Statements about differentiation	Your order	Justify your order in terms of contribution to the inclusive classroom
a. All children work at their own individual level on different assignments within a given topic.		
b. Teach to the middle; give the same materials (books, worksheets, assignments, questions) to all pupils.		
c. Divide the class into ability groups; set different work (within the same topic area) to each ability group.		
d. Teach to the middle as in (b) but give extension work to the most able.		
e. Grade questions and assignments so that only the more able pupils get to the more demanding aspects of the topic.		
f. Set the same, very open assignments to all children which can be interpreted at different levels.		
g. Tasks selected by pupils themselves from a given range.		
h. Same assignment for all pupils, but in groups pupils help each other.		
i. Give the same book or set of worksheets to all pupils, but they work through them at different rates.		
j. Core and options. All pupils attempt some aspects of the topic unit and then have a range of differentiated choices.		

Further reading

Hartas, D. (2004) 'Special Educational Needs and Inclusive Schooling', in Brooks, V, Abbott, I. and Bills, L. (eds) *Preparing to Teach in Secondary Schools*. Buckingham: Open University Press.

Harrison, C., Simon, S. and Watson, R. (2000) 'Progression and Differentiation', in Monk, M. and Osborne, J. (eds) *Good Practice in Science Teaching*. Buckingham: Open University Press.

Peterson, S., Williams, J. and Sorensen, P. (2000) 'Science for All: the challenge of inclusion' in Sears, J. and Sorensen, P. (eds) *Issues in Science Teaching*. London: Routledge.

4 Assessment in science

By the end of this chapter you should have considered and reflected upon:

- **what** is understood by assessment in the secondary school curriculum;
- **why** assessment needs to be considered when developing learning and teaching episodes for science in secondary schools;
- **how** learning and teaching episodes, in science, can be developed which have assessment for learning embedded.

Linking your learning
Achieving QTS Reflective Reader: Secondary Professional Studies. Hoult, S. (2005) Chapter 6

Professional Standards for QTS
3.1.1, 3.2.1, 3.2.2, 3.2.4

Introduction

The *Oxford English Dictionary* (OED), defines *assessment* as:

> *The process or means of evaluating academic work; an examination or test.*

This is often a common view shared by trainee (and some experienced) teachers. What we will argue in this chapter is that assessment is much more than this. Assessment, we contend, is an integral part of learning and teaching which can both help pupils learning, by giving clear targets, and enable teachers to plan.

You will reflect on both *formative* and *summative* assessment. In addition you will reflect on the *reliability* and *validity* of assessment instruments. The intended outcome is that you develop a sense of purpose for your assessment strategy which goes beyond that of simply evaluating.

Growing up in Derbyshire, a common saying amongst sheep farmers was:

> *If you want a sheep to grow then feed it don't weigh it!*

It is this 'feeding the mind' approach to assessment which we hope to convey in the text and activities of the chapter. This approach is echoed by Ofsted (2003) when they write:

> *Assessment is most effective where it is used as a teaching tool as well as a means of judging attainment. Much secondary science involves abstract ideas and an important function of assessment is to enable teachers to discover what point pupils have reached*

in their own understanding of these ideas. Similarly the assessment of practical course-work is not just a means of assigning pupils to levels but of giving them the information they need to improve their laboratory skills.

The point about the assessment of practical work is addressed in Chapter 5, 'Planning and assessing investigations in science'.

What

So, what is it that we mean when we talk about assessment? Our first task is to break the definition into two distinct parts, formative and summative assessment.

Formative assessment (or assessment for learning; see later) can be taken to be diagnostic in nature which, with feedback from the teacher, helps both pupil and teacher plan for the next steps in the pupil's future development.

> *If feedback is not acted upon the activity could not be regarded as genuinely formative.*
>
> (Sadler, 1989)

Summative assessment can be taken to be the test or examination which gives the pupils a grade or level. This is often, at Key Stages 3 and 4, judging pupils against a national standard, for example SATs (levels) and GCSEs (grades).

Unfortunately, however, not all aspects of a pupil's science experience are assessable and often those aspects which are assessable assume some degree of hierarchy over those which are not.

When we make an assessment, be it formative or summative, we need to ask two questions of the instrument we use: are the data generated valid and reliable? The *reliability* of the data refers to the ability of two or more teachers (assessors) being able to arrive at the same mark, grade or level for a given pupil. Variation in the results of a test, its reliability, can be explained under four main headings:

- The pupil: performance varies from task to task, from question to question. The interaction of the pupil with the task set is 'by far the greatest source of variation' (Satterly, 1994)
- The assessor: a clear mark scheme (see later in this chapter) should limit this effect but differences between assessors will exist to some extent. It is also the case that if the same marker re-marks a piece of work they may not arrive at the same outcome.
- The assessment instrument: by making the test more objective and less subjective, higher levels of reliability can be obtained. The trade-off here is, however, a reduction in validity.
- The situation: the conditions under which the assessment is carried out should be standardised, i.e. candidates have the same access to resources, same time limits and are under the same physical conditions.

The *validity* of an assessment instrument refers to the ability of the instrument (test or examination) to test what you are trying to assess. In science, two issues often arise which may challenge the validity of an assessment:

- Literacy: in written tests, or examinations, regardless of our intent the candidate must be able to read the question, extract the relevant information and write an appropriate response. If the aim is to test a pupils understanding of Ohm's Law, should literacy also be assessed?
- Numeracy: as with literacy, a number of science assessments rapidly become a test of mathematical skill, with little requirement on science understanding, which raises the question, should we be assessing mathematics in a science assessment?

In Key Stage 3 SATs the validity could also be questioned on the group of coverage. If all three years of the programme of study (PoS) are to be assessed, how can this be done in a single paper taking one hour?

It should be manifest that reliability and validity are interrelated and in reality a compromise needs to be achieved.

Personal response

How does the view of assessment given above match with your expectations?

Practical implications and activities

- With your school-based mentor examine the departmental policy on assessment. How well does it match with the whole school policy?

- Does the policy balance formative and summative assessments?

- By looking at marked work, in books and tests, how well does the policy match practice?

Why

Given the above, we can ask the question: why do we assess? We will argue that the systematic use of assessment is essential for planning. Ofsted (2003) say that it is most effective when it 'influences medium or long-term planning'.

Three aspects of why we assess, which will be revisited later in this chapter, are given below:

- to evaluate our teaching methodology;
- to set targets, via formative feedback;
- to inform and guide our professional judgements of pupils.

Returning to the notion of formative and summative assessment, it can be argued that:

Formative assessment is generally defined as taking place during a course with the express purpose of improving pupil learning.

(Torrance and Pryor, 1998)

All we do in the classroom or laboratory should carry the aim of improving pupil learning and hence, if for no other reason, assessment has an important role to play. The DfES (2002) write, to this end:

assessment is one of the most powerful tools for promoting learning and raising standards.

The term 'formative assessment' is replaced by DfES (2002) with 'assessment for learning', which is defined as:

where pupils' progress is judged against their targets and the next steps in their learning clarified.

Formative assessment therefore has its *raison d'être* firmly in the development of pupils' learning. Alternatively, summative assessment appears to serve a very different master:

Summative assessment is generally considered to be undertaken at the end of a course or programme of study in order to measure and communicate pupil performance for purposes of certification and (latterly) accountability.

(Torrance and Pryor, 1998)

The emphasis on certification and accountability takes away much of the developmental nature of the assessment and may lead to some 'teaching to the test'. In the UK the use of school league tables and threshold payments both serve to drive certification and accountability at the cost, some would argue, of deep understanding:

More departments are now generating numerical measures of progress. These are often based on internal or published test scores from which incremental nation curriculum levels are calculated.

(Ofsted, 2003)

Remember the sheep? If you want it to grow then feed it, don't weigh it. This is not, however, to trivialise summative assessment since the certification gained by pupils will impact on their progression from GCSE to A-level and from A-level to further or higher education by either a vocational or academic route.

Personal response

Why do you think we should assess pupils?
Where would you see yourself on the question of formative and summative assessment?

Practical implications and activities

- With your school-based mentor, revisit the departmental assessment policy. How is the emphasis on formative and summative assessment set out?

- By revisiting pupils' work, how does the practice match policy?

How

In this section you will reflect on the previous two and start to put into practice strategies for formative assessment and summative assessment which goes beyond certification.

Before you read the following extract, read:

- Brooks, V. (2004) 'Using Assessment for Formative Purposes' in Brooks, V. et al. *Preparing to Teach in Secondary Schools* (pages 109–122). Buckingham: Open University Press.

Extract: Brooks, V. (2002) *Assessment in Secondary Schools.* **Open University Press. Pages 64–67.**

Black and Wiliam (1998a: 12–13) cite a study which investigated the effects of three different feedback types on pupils' subsequent achievements and motivation. The pupils were given a series of tasks to complete and at the end of each pair of tasks they were given feedback before embarking on the next pair:

- one-third of the group received individually composed comments on the level of match between their work and the assessment criteria which had been described to all beforehand;
- another third were given grades only;
- the final group received a grade and a comment.

When asked to predict which feedback type produced the best results in terms of improving pupils' subsequent performances and motivation, most people believe that it is the third (grade + comment) which is the most efficacious. In fact, the only group which managed to raise its performance and then to sustain the improvement over the series of tasks was the 'comments only' group. The 'grades + comments' group showed a steady decline in performance across the tasks whereas the 'grades only' group showed an initial improvement in performance which was not sustained. Pupils' interest in the work followed a similar pattern to their attainment with one exception. The pupils who took part in this marking experiment were drawn from various classes in different schools. However, they were selected on the basis of ability, either because they were among the highest achievers in their class or because they were among the lowest attainers. It was found that high achievers maintained a high level of interest in the tasks irrespective of the type of feedback they received. However, both feedback systems which entailed giving grades undermined the original level of interest displayed by low achievers.

Several qualifications need to be borne in mind when considering the implications of these findings. They are derived from a single study based on a marking experiment which was not related to pupils' normal curriculum and was not carried out by their regular teachers. This raises questions about the extent to which the findings can be generalised to ordinary classrooms. However, these reservations have to be set against the equally serious questions about conventional marking practices which this study raises in its findings that:

- different feedback types had a differential impact on subsequent performance (grading was associated with a decline in performance for both groups who were exposed to it);
- different feedback types affected motivation differently for high and low achievers (grading was associated with a loss of interest in work among low attainers);
- the effects of grading were more potent than the effects of constructive written feedback (even when feedback tailored to individuals' needs was provided, its formative potential appeared to be undermined by the presence of grades).

Most people find these results disconcerting because they conflict with established wisdom about good professional practice. This may result in the findings being dismissed out of hand, just as pupils have difficulty in accepting new concepts which clash with existing ideas (for example John's belief in Chapter 1 that everything that trees are made of comes out of the ground). However, these findings should at least give us pause for thought and cause us to question the prominence attributed to scoring in conventional marking procedures. There is other evidence which points to a similar conclusion: that *conventional marking practices simply don't work!*

> even when teachers provide students with valid and reliable judgments about the quality of their work, improvement does not necessarily follow. Students often show little or no growth or development despite regular, accurate feedback.
>
> (Sadler 1989: 119)

> Even when teachers' comments on work are thorough and point the way to improvement, pupils often do not engage with or respond to them. Corrections are frequently not made. Inadequate work is seldom improved. Even when pupils attempt to respond to comments, teachers do not sufficiently acknowledge this when next marking their books. The full potential of marking to support progress is rarely capitalised upon.
>
> (Ofsted 1998a: 93)

When we add to this the tracts of teachers' time and energy that marking absorbs, the conclusion that it is time for a radical rethink of approaches to marking is further reinforced.

Your ability to think and act radically is, of course, constrained by your status as a trainee. If there is an agreed marking policy operating in your placement department/ school, you should normally comply with it. If a laissez-faire approach pertains, allowing you discretion, you should resist the temptation simply to adopt the practices with which you are familiar from your own education without subjecting these practices to careful scrutiny. The challenge is to provide the kind of feedback which persuades pupils to engage thoughtfully with its messages and then to translate that engagement into improved performance.

Perhaps the first thing to challenge, however, is the notion of 'marking'. It is a curiously inexact term which may suggest the making of marks on scripts, annotating them with codes and strokes. It may also suggest the process of arriving at a mark. The conventional mark book, full of tiny squares big enough to accommodate only numbers and symbols, reinforces this impression. In contrast, this chapter examines approaches to feedback in which the provision of a mark may have no part to play. This is why the chapter is entitled 'Ways of responding to pupils' written and practical work' not 'Marking . . . work'. Although the term 'marking' is too deeply embedded in teaching culture to be ousted, it is worth acknowledging that it is an imprecise, catch-all term and potentially misleading. Indeed, one study of how mentors presented assessment to student teachers found that: 'More commonly, the term "assessment" was used to mean marking [with an emphasis on its] summative function . . . Homework was most frequently explained as a necessity which teachers set to meet the expectations of others, with the marking fulfilling a policing function' (Butterfield et al. 1999: 238 and 232).

Analysis

The extract may, at first, to be counter-intuitive – all pupils want grades, don't they? It would appear that this is not the case unless the pupil is consistently getting high grades. Hence for the majority of pupils the comments written are more important than the grade and we would argue that even for the high achievers, comments which set targets for progression are beneficial.

If we do not wish to undermine the formative aspect of written comments, we should consider avoiding grades. This approach is achievable in the majority of what we do with class work, homework and in-class 'tests'. With external assessments, for example SATs, GCSE and A-levels, ultimately a grade needs to be given but all practice and 'mock' papers should also carry formative comments. In order to maintain pupil interest there is also a good case for limiting the use of assessment instruments which require a grade or level. To this end the Assessment Reform Group (1999), in *Assessment for Learning – Beyond the Black Box,* propose that assessment for learning (formative assessment) should:

- be embedded in the teaching and learning and not a separate task;
- involve sharing lesson objectives with pupils;
- aim to help pupils to know the standards they are aiming for;
- involve pupils in self-assessment;
- provide feedback to pupils so that they recognise their next steps in learning and how to take them;
- involve pupils and teachers reviewing and reflecting on assessment data.

Whilst the above looks at written work and appropriate formative responses, the use of oral questions should not be underestimated as a formative (or indeed summative) tool. However, we would urge caution in simply firing questions to the class. Key questions and expected answers should be part of your planning. Questions to be asked should be differentiated and geared towards an inclusive classroom (see Chapter 3). The following pointers are offered to develop your questioning skills:

- avoid the temptation to prompt the answer;
- allow thinking time between the question and the first response;
- always look for something positive in every response;
- rather than 'give' an answer after a response adopt a 'that's nearly there, can someone help her out?' approach;
- ensure everyone is included by using both open and directed questions;
- consider using groups or pairs to discuss a question before requiring an answer.

Personal response

Thinking back to your own school, college or university assessments, did you look at the grade, read the comments, or both?

If you only received a grade, good or bad, what effect did it have on your interest in the subject and motivation to improve?

Practical implications and activities

As a trainee or newly qualified teacher you need to demonstrate your ability to set and evaluate pupils work. The following activities are designed to help you meet the appropriate standards and, perhaps more importantly, enhance pupils' learning in science.

Questioning:
- With a trainee colleague or mentor, plan a question-and-answer session for the start of a lesson.
- Whilst you deliver the lesson, ask your partner to observe your performance against the questioning skills above.
- In another lesson arrange to exchange roles.

Written work:
- With your school-based mentor, plan a lesson which includes a written homework task.
- In your plan make sure that the learning objectives (see Chapter 1) are shared with the class.
- When you assess the submitted work avoid using grades and make sure that your comments link back to the learning objectives.
- Finally, ask the pupils to comment on the feedback they received.

Test or examination:
In order to maintain reliability and validity, a mark scheme needs to be developed for a test.

- Either using a standard test or by devising one of you own, write your answers to the questions.
- Decide how many of the marks for each question will be given to each step or point.
- Have a group sit the test and mark five, at random, against your mark scheme.
- Do the pupils' answers match your expected answers or does the mark scheme need adjusting?
- Use your adjusted mark scheme to mark all scripts and discuss the outcomes with your mentor.
- Finally, write targets for development on the scripts before returning them to the pupils.

Record-keeping:
In order to make more effective, use of grades from tests and to evaluate the tests themselves ICT becomes a useful ally.

- By putting marks in a spreadsheet, both pupil performance and the performance of the test instrument can be monitored. In addition, targets for feedback to pupils can be developed in this way.
- During your school-based practice develop an electronic mark book which allows you to evaluate the performance of both pupils and instruments. At the end of the practice share and discuss your findings with your mentor.

Further reading

Brooks, V. (2002) *Assessment in Secondary Schools.* Buckingham: Open University Press.

Torrance, H. and Pryor, J. (1998) *Investigating Formative Assessment.* Buckingham: Open University Press.

5 Planning and assessing investigations in science

By the end of this chapter you should have considered and reflected upon:

- **what** is understood by the term investigation in secondary school science;
- **why** investigations should be integrated into learning and teaching episodes for science in secondary schools;
- **how** investigations can be planned, implemented and assessed.

Linking your learning
Achieving QTS Reflective Reader: Primary Science. Hoult, S. (2005) Chapter 4.

Professional Standards for QTS
2.1c, 2.1d, 3.1.3, 3.2.3, 3.3.2c, 3.3.2d, 3.3.8

Introduction

Practical work, experimental work and investigative work – are they all the same? We would suggest not and we would further suggest the term 'experiment' is too often misused in schools.

> *Year after year, this same teacher makes his students perform the same experiments. Well, if the experiments have been done so many times before, how can they still be experiments?*
>
> (Martin, 1990)

How often do we see, or did you experience, something along the lines of, 'today we are going to do an experiment to prove Hooke's Law (or Ohm's Law)?' Are these really experiments? If they are worded as given here then we would say not, but this does not stop them being experiments for the pupils. In this case we need to have an important prerequisite: the pupils should not have the answer prior to carrying it out. The lesson could then become: 'today you are going to investigate the effect of adding a load to a spring'. With guidance this is then an experiment where pupils can predict, collect data, analyse data and draw conclusions. For us, investigations take a step further: often the teacher does not know the answer (often there isn't one) and pupils can work to their own plan.

In this chapter we will explore the many facets of investigative work in the secondary science curriculum, including the assistance we can give to pupils and the ways in which investigative work may be assessed.

What

It is difficult to define what an investigation is.

> *Lack of clarity of definition has bedevilled (and still does bedevil) education in general and science education in particular.*
>
> (Gott and Duggan, 1995)

Within the National Curriculum for England (DfEE, 1999) at Key Stage 3 pupils are, under the umbrella term 'investigative skills', expected to be taught:

- planning;
- obtaining and presenting evidence;
- considering evidence;
- evaluating.

For 2006 the programme of study for Key Stage 4 (DfES, 2006), under the umbrella term 'how science works', requires pupils to be taught:

- data, evidence, theories and explanations;
- practical and enquiry skills;
- communication skills;
- applications and implications of science.

The National Curriculum for Wales (ACCAC, 2000) makes similar, but not identical, requirements. For example, at Key Stage 4 pupils should be taught:

- planning experimental procedures;
- obtaining evidence;
- analysing information;
- evaluating information.

A consensus view is that investigations require some degree, from the pupils, of planning, carrying out, analysis and evaluation – not really a definition of an investigation but a good description. However, investigations share two other common attributes: variables and questions. They require the manipulation of variables; Foulds and Gott (1988) have used variables to generate a typology of investigations, as shown in Table 5.1.

Table 5.1 A typology of investigations

Question	Example
A single categoric variable	Which is the best type of insulation for a hot water tank?
A single continuous variable	Find out how the rate at which the water cools is dependent on the amount of water in the tank
More than one independent variable	Is it the type of insulation material or its thickness which is keeping the water hot?
Constructional activities	Make the best insulated hot water tank

In addition to the manipulation of variables, an investigation needs a question to investigate. Wellington (2002) presents a framework for reflecting on types of investigation. The framework is based on three axes, each on a continuum, upon which each investigation can be mapped. This is shown in Figure 5.1.

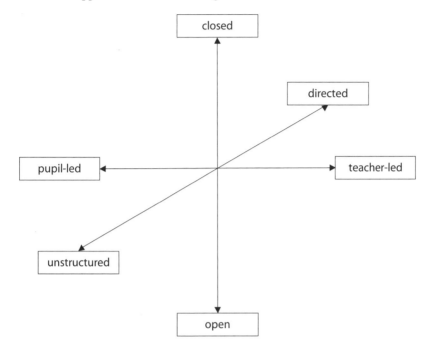

Figure 5.1 Dimensions of investigative work

An *investigation* can be taken as a learning and teaching episode which requires pupils to plan an approach to addressing a problem, obtaining and analysing data before drawing conclusions on these data and evaluating the outcome. It should be noted that an investigation is not the same as *investigative skills*. The skills can be taught and developed outside the context of a full investigation, for example, analysing a given data set or planning an investigation which the school does not have the resources to implement.

Personal response

How would you define an investigation in science?
Thinking back to your time at school do you now think you carried out any investigations?

Practical implications and activities

With your school based mentor, or a colleague, review the school's scheme of work for science, at either Key Stage 3 or Key Stage 4, and discuss the opportunities available for pupils to carry out investigative work.

Why

One reason that pupils undertake investigations in science at Key Stages 3 and 4, is that they are part of the National Curriculum for both England and Wales.

It is also true that in order to achieve Qualified Teacher Status (QTS) trainees are required to demonstrate the following:

> *For Key Stage 3, they know and understand the relevant National Curriculum Programme(s) of Study, and for those qualifying to teach one or more of the core subjects, the relevant frameworks, methods and expectations set out in the National Strategy for Key Stage 3.*

> *They are able to assess pupils' progress accurately using, as relevant, the Early Learning Goals, National Curriculum Level Descriptions, criteria from national qualifications, the requirements of Awarding Bodies, National Curriculum and Foundation Stage assessment frameworks or objectives from the national strategies.*

> (DfEE, 2002)

However, there is something more than this pragmatic reason to using investigations in school science. For a number of pupils investigations are the thing that turns them on to science. Investigations can help develop group work and communication skills, both part of the citizenship requirements. For teachers it provides an avenue to try alternative teaching approaches. Using small groups and active learning through the context of the investigation can serve as a motivator to continue with science and study the content.

> *An emphasis on the use of practical work and on working in small groups may improve attitudes to science, but unless there is an increase in the amount of active learning, it is unlikely to be an effective motivator.*

> (Brichenco et al., 2000)

The above statement supports the view that practical or experimental work needs to be made investigative, thus creating a climate of active learning to motivate pupils; see Chapter 3.

Personal response

Thinking back to your own learning in school, why do you think practical or investigative work was done?

Looking ahead to your own teaching, why do think you should include investigative work in your science teaching?

Practical implications and activities

After observing a practical session in school, discuss with your school-based mentor why investigative work is included in the school's scheme of work in science:

- Does the reasoning go beyond the National Curriculum or examination requirements? What pedagogical reasons are offered?

- Taking one of the school's Key Stage 3 investigations, can you place it on the three-dimensional space shown in Figure 5.1?

How

If investigations can serve as generic motivators and allow pupils to access the science content through context-led teaching, it is difficult to argue against their inclusion. What is more difficult, however, is answering two 'how?' questions: how do you set an investigation? How do you assess an investigation?

This section aims to address both of these questions, with an emphasis on Key Stage 3. However, the principles transfer to Key Stages 4 and 5.

In setting pupils an investigative task you must first be clear that they understand what it means to investigate. An investigation can be seen as a cyclical process for which pupils can be given ownership. Allowing pupils, with guidance, to define what is required at each stage can give them that ownership. Figure 5.2 shows an example investigation cycle which can be used with pupils, taking their consensus view to fill in the boxes.

Having explored how to investigate, pupils require an interesting context to investigate, an *investigation brief*. Consider the following two questions:

1. What are the factors that affect the cooking of pasta?
2. Mario and Marco both claim to be able to cook the fastest macaroni in their restaurants. A competition is arranged and your group has been employed (by either Mario or Marco) to advise on the fastest method. What advice will you give?

Both questions require the same investigation of the variables temperature, size of macaroni and ratio of water to macaroni in the pan. But think, as an average 14-year-old, which would you be most drawn to answering?

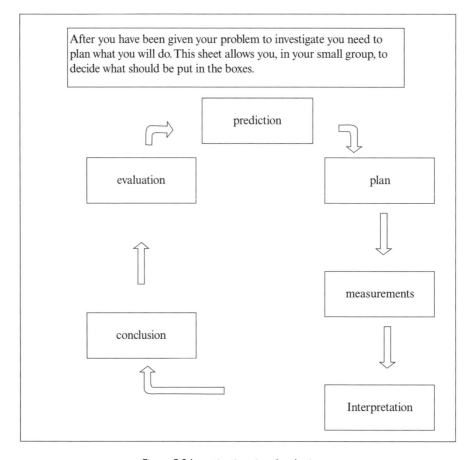

After you have been given your problem to investigate you need to plan what you will do. This sheet allows you, in your small group, to decide what should be put in the boxes.

prediction

evaluation

plan

measurements

conclusion

Interpretation

Figure 5.2 Investigations in school science

In attempting the macaroni investigation pupils could be required to make a presentation to the class and a competition could be arranged. Furthermore, colleagues from food technology could be involved – the quickest may not be best in terms of nutrition (or indeed taste).

Having pupils work in a small group does not automatically mean you have to assess them as a group. Each pupil can be required to present an individual report which, with a little imagination, can go beyond the 'title, diagram, method, results and conclusion' approach common in many school practicals.

It should not be expected that pupils are able to plan an investigation without guidance, nor should it be the case that pupils who fail to produce a workable plan or collect usable data are barred from scoring highly in other aspects of the investigation. We suggest that prompt sheets be available for all aspects of the investigation; for example, Figures 5.3 provides sample prompt sheets for planning an investigation and for those who fail to collect useable data.

In assessing Key Stage 3 investigations we are looking for evidence of:

- planning;
- obtaining and presenting evidence;
- considering evidence;
- evaluating;

and assigning a level using the level descriptors given in the National Curriculum.

This makes it harder than Key Stage 4, where examination groups offer more clearly defined descriptors, with numerical scores, for each skill area. You are advised to study carefully the assessment criteria for the GCSE courses in the school in which you are placed.

Looking for evidence against each skill is the first step, but eventually you must arrive at a 'best-fit' level for the pupil, based on the descriptors. For example at Level 3 at Key Stage 3, the National Curriculum for England states that a pupil should be able to:

respond to suggestions and put forward their own ideas about how to find the answer to a question. They recognise why it is important to collect data to answer questions. They use simple texts to find information. They make relevant observations and measure quantities, such as length or mass, using a range of simple equipment. Where appropriate, they carry out a fair test with some help, recognising and explaining why it is fair. They record their observations in a variety of ways. They provide explanations for observations and for simple patterns in recorded measurements. They communicate in a scientific way what they have found out and suggest improvements in their work.

(DfEE, 1999, p. 75)

At Level 7 they should be able to:

describe some predictions based on scientific theories and give examples of the evidence collected to test these predictions. In their own work, they use scientific knowledge and understanding to decide on appropriate approaches to questions. They identify the key factors in complex contexts and in contexts in which variables cannot readily be controlled, and plan appropriate procedures. They synthesise information from a range of sources, and identify possible limitations in secondary data. They make systematic observations and measurements with precision, using a wide range of apparatus. They identify when they need to repeat measurements, comparisons and observations in order to obtain reliable data. Where appropriate, they represent data in graphs, using lines of best fit. They draw conclusions that are consistent with the evidence and explain these using scientific knowledge and understanding. They begin to consider whether the data they have collected are sufficient for the conclusions they have drawn. They communicate what they have done using a wide range of scientific and technical language and conventions, including symbols and flow diagrams.

(DfEE, 1999, p. 75)

When we consider evaluation of investigative work, the level decriptors in the National Curriculum are not written in pupil-friendly language and so the opportunities for self-assessment are limited. One strategy to encourage both self-assessment and a

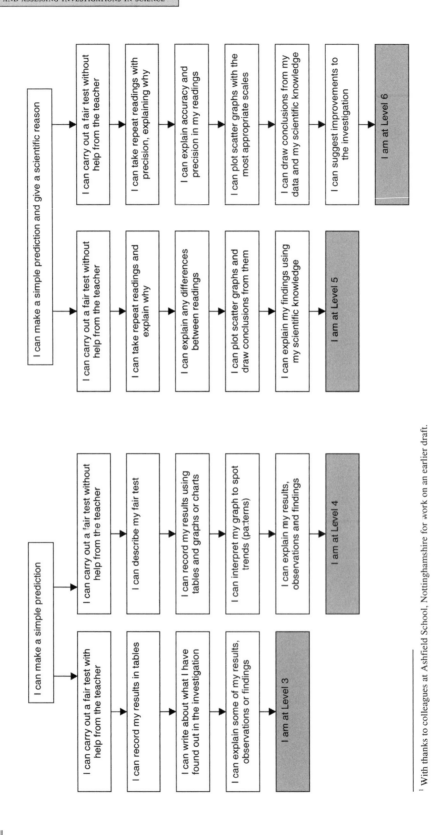

Figure 5.3 Self assessment sheet for investigations I at Key Stage 3

[1] With thanks to colleagues at Ashfield School, Nottinghamshire for work on an earlier draft.

greater understanding of the assessment criteria is to reword the descriptors in pupil-friendly language, perhaps using the pupils to help develop the statements. Figure 5.3 offers an example of a self-assessment sheet for Key Stage 3 covering Levels 3 to 6.

However, it is not always the case that 'hands-on' practicals need be used to engage pupils. The following extract suggests alternatives for practical work.

Extract: Osborne, J. (1997) Practical alternatives in *School Science Review* Vol 78 No. 285. Pages 61–67.

Abstract

It is argued that the doing and learning of science are not the same thing and that practical work only forms one strategy in an effective teacher's repertoire. Strategies are suggested, involving active learning of a non-practical nature, which encourage discussion of science by children working in small groups. These activities have been shown to engage pupils' interest and provide effective learning tools. Some examples of less familiar practical alternatives are described.

Improvements in science education are, in my opinion, most likely to come from making an important distinction between *doing* science and *learning* science. The two are not one and the same thing. The former is necessary to discover and establish new knowledge of the natural and living world but, just as writing poetry is not the best way to learn poetry, neither is the almost ritualistic emphasis on doing science, prevalent in science classrooms, the best way to learn science. In the *learning* of science, practical work only forms one strategy in an extended repertoire. Just as the golfer carefully selects the best club to suit his or her needs, so in teaching science, particularly in secondary schools, children benefit from teachers who carefully choose *learning strategies* that are demonstrably the most appropriate and effective.

Evidence is beginning to mount that effective teachers select their classroom activities from an extensive armoury, picking those that are most likely to hit their target. In the words of the Scottish HMI (1994), the key to success lies in the use of '*a variety of learning and teaching strategies*'. After painstaking and detailed research into effective teaching and learning, Cooper and McIntyre (1996, p. 131) also concluded that:

> *Effective teaching, it would seem, is more likely to depend on the teacher's mastery of a wide range of strategies (e.g. from transmission to self-direction) and, importantly, the ability to evaluate circumstances that render the application of a particular strategy appropriate to student requirements. Sometimes a global strategy for whole groups will be appropriate, and may require the teacher to engage in transmission style; at other times more student-directed approaches will be appropriate.*

This article suggests a few strategies that teachers might add to their repertoire to encourage children to talk about scientific ideas and reflect on their own understanding, based around working in small groups. When most teachers spend their time trying to diminish classroom chatter, why might such activities be beneficial?

In most classroom discussions, the teacher asks the questions, a pupil responds and then the teacher provides an evaluation with feedback (Lemke, 1990; Edwards and Mercer, 1987). This form of dialogue is not only severely restricted but, on reflection, somewhat perverse. In the science classroom, questions are asked, surprisingly, not by those who *do not* know, but by the teacher who *does*. Moreover, questions are often closed and the average time teachers wait for a response rarely exceeds three seconds (Rowe, 1974). Thus, not only do the unfortunate pupils have minimal time to even gather their thoughts but, more importantly, the focus of interest is not determined by the pupils' questions and what they want to know. This state of affairs is of concern in the light of Cooper and McIntyre's findings that the most effective forms of teaching are 'interactive' or 'reactive' styles where pupils' inputs are valued and teaching is based on teachers' perceptions of student concerns and interest.

Many children are reluctant to engage in such discourse in classrooms for fear of exposing their ignorance. In contrast, real science is an exciting cultural product where ideas are introduced, discussed and explained through dialogue with peers and there is opportunity for critical questioning and elaboration. It is only when you are required to explain a concept in words to somebody else that you really start to understand it. Learning a science is akin to learning a foreign language: words in science have a set of associated relationships and legitimate contexts. Recognising the distinction in the meaning of the word 'force' in the sentences *'The force of gravity acts on the apple'* and *'May the force be with you'* comes only by asking children to use the appropriate language in the appropriate context. What then can be done to provide such opportunities for children to engage in open and unrestricted discourse about science in a non-threatening atmosphere? It is here that small-group work has an vital role to play.

Working in small groups
Traditionally, this technique has been underused in science teaching. Sands' (1981) investigation of the use of group work in school science concluded that:

> No opportunity was given to groups to design experiments or interpret results. If there was any imaginative, analytical thought-provoking or enquiry-based thinking it was done by the teacher with the whole class... Rarely was there a follow-up related to the group work involving a sharing of experience. What few follow-ups were observed were used for putting results from each group on the blackboard with a brief summary, or giving instructions about dealing with results and writing up.

Moreover, those interactions that did take place within the groups were at a relatively low cognitive level. Sands concluded that meaningful group work was more of a myth than a reality. Little seems to have changed, as the Office for Standards in Education recently noted: 'small group activities, other than for practical work, are very uncommon' (OFSTED, 1995). Despite a major transformation in examinations, the introduction of broad and balanced science and the advent of a National Curriculum in England and Wales with an ambitious and novel model of practical science embodied in Sc1, this aspect of science teaching remains unchanged – evidently a case of 'plus ça change, plus c'est la même chose'.

Small groups provide a context for structured exercises that constrain and conscript children to a well-defined task, easing the management and organisational difficulties of operating within a classroom. Most importantly, they provide an ideal forum for exploring the knowledge of the child and developing their understanding, for example by exploring the relationship between what they know and the evidence for its justification. It is only when called upon to explain, for example, how you know that plants make their own food through photosynthesis, that electric current is conserved in a circuit or that matter is conserved in combustion, that the crucial significance of experimental evidence is exposed. This feature is at the heart of the rationale of science and has enabled science to achieve such success. Reasoning in science requires discussion in a non-threatening and non-judgmental atmosphere involving the constructive criticism which only peer group discussion in small groups affords. Such work provides a valuable opportunity for the child to *integrate her capacities and interpretations with those of significant others around her* (Bruner and Haste, 1987).

Possibly the most familiar use of small-group work is to produce posters for presentation to peers, explaining an experimental investigation or the results of research into a set topic. Although time consuming, the seriousness with which children approach such work and the quality of the work can often astonish. Some less familiar techniques based on small-group work, which share a similar potential to stimulate discussion and *talk about* science, are described below.

Discussion of instances/misconceptions

The extensive body of literature on children's thinking hat has been produced in the past 15 years provides a valuable source of common errors and misconceptions which can be posed to students for discussion in small groups (Figure 1). Pupils should initially be asked to work through the statements in the left-hand column of Figure 1 individually, deciding whether they agree or disagree with the statements. They should also be encouraged to use the final column to provide notes on evidence for their beliefs. Then, having completed the first stage of their task, and only then, should pupils be allowed to discuss their thinking on each of the topics and come to some common agreement. Rarely do they agree and the ensuing discussion is often heated. Pupils should be encouraged to draw on whatever resources are available, such as books, CD-ROMs, posters and models, to help justify their pinions and views so that the activity is a stimulus or learning.

Statement	Agree	Disagree	Evidence/Reasons
A man lost one of his fingers in an accident. If he has a child afterwards, how many fingers will his children have?			
A naturalist carried out an experiment consisting of cutting off the tails of mice through several generations to see how the offspring come out. What do you think would happen over 20 generations?			
Mr and Mrs Cross have three boys. They are sure that their next child will be a boy. Would you agree?			
A gardener uses the pollen of a blue lupin to pollinate another blue lupin. Does this mean that all the seeds from this plant will produce blue lupins?			
Is there anything wrong with this statement? 'My father's genes must be stronger than my mother's because I inherit so much of my looks from him.'			
Carol has a flat nose similar to her aunt. Both her parents have prominent noses but all four of her grandparents have flat noses. Is this possible?			
A boy is much more likely to look like his father than his mother.			

Figure 1 Statements for discussion

This technique is easily adapted to other topics, for example:

- astronomy – 'it is hotter in summer as we are nearer the sun';
- photosynthesis – 'plants get their food from the soil';
- motion – 'a bicycle slows down because it runs out of force to keep it going'.

All that is necessary is to take the many common misconceptions that children have and ask them to discuss whether they are true or false. When the groups have concluded their discussions, they are much more receptive to the scientific view as they want to know and to resolve any disagreement with their peers.

An important aspect of this strategy is that it offers a means of exploring the epistemological question of *how we know*. Sc 2–4 of the National Curriculum can be viewed as a survey of the facts of science – focusing on 'what we know'. It is possible to teach just this component and justify its importance in terms of the utilitarian value of such knowledge, but to do so is to rely solely on persuasion and authority. Science courses that fail to consider the important dimension of how scientists come to know *'are running the risk of developing students who do not acknowledge the scientist's views as rational'* (Duschl, 1990), for where is the evidence that justifies the science teacher's beliefs? For instance, everybody knows that day and night are caused by a spinning Earth rather then a moving Sun, but how many individuals can tell you the evidence for such a belief? Without such evidence, how are the grounds for beliefs discussed in the school laboratories of the developed world any different from those offered to the child in the African village? As Horton (1967) points out: *'In both cases the propounders are deferred to as the accredited agents of tradition.'*

Jumbled sentences

This simple technique provides an exercise where pupils have to work out as many correct sentences as they can from several jumbled ones, as in Figure 2. They are allowed to pick one word or phrase from each column to make up their sentence which must form a correct scientific proposition. Pupils should work in small groups and discuss the acceptability of the statements they suggest for possible sentences.

Figure 3 shows another version with a different focus. The task can be given a competitive element by challenging groups to produce the largest number of sentences they can, which adds an additional element of enjoyment for many pupils.

Instructions
Make at least seven true sentences by choosing an entry from each column. The same words can be used in more than one sentence.

	atom			a	and	
All	matter		not	many	charged	atom/s
An	electron shell	is	found	protons	in	nucleus
The	electron	is not	composed of	in	a/an	particle/s
A	atomic		made up of	orbiting	the	neutron/s
	nucleus			electrons	small	orbit
	neutron			two kinds of	electrons	

Figure 2 Jumbled sentences

Instructions

Make as many correct sentences as you can using words from each column. The same words can be used in more than one sentence.

An electron	is	the	number	who showed that most of the atom was empty space.
J J Thomson	was	a	Greek	that shows the total number of nuclear participles.
The nucleus	is	a	New Zealand scientist	who stated that matter was made up of atoms.
The atomic number	was	an	atomic particle	that has a positive charge.
Democritus	is	a	scientist	of the atom and is made up of protons and neutrons.
Rutherford	is	a	central part	that is negatively charged and orbits the nucleus.
A proton	is	the	number	
The mass number	was	a	nuclear particle	that shows the total number of protons.

Figure 3 Another example of jumbled sentences

Instructions

Bob Fair, a year 10 pupil, was given the words in boxes and drew this concept map. Write down the errors which Bob has made.

Redraw the concept map correctly.

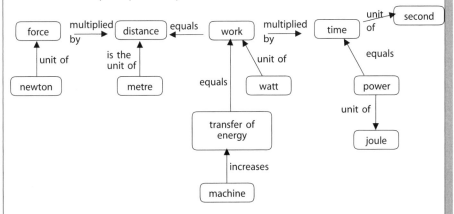

Figure 4 A false concept map

The false concept map

The value of concept maps – essentially diagrams which contain a limited number of 'concepts' with the propositional relationships which join them written on linking arrows – for learning and teaching have been discussed extensively (Novak and Gowin, 1984; Osborne, 1993; Adamzyk et al., 1994). Recent research (Sizmur, 1994) has shown that group concept mapping provides significant opportunities for children to have elaborated dialogue about science – that is to question each other's ideas and interpret their meaning to one another. Another valuable technique for promoting useful discussion is to present children with a concept map which deliberately contains a number of fallacious propositions as in Figure 4. Here some of the relations are true and some are false. The challenge to the pupils is to find all the errors in the map, and then to redraw the map correctly. Once again, asking pupils to work in small groups of three or four provides an opportunity to discuss and question the propositions and to justify their reasoning to each other. Such an activity takes 20 to 30 minutes and is valuable as an informal exercise to assess how well a topic has been understood.

Conclusions

The message underpinning these examples of practical alternatives is a belief that children are curious and will engage with science if they are encouraged to ask questions and discuss possible answers. Watts and Alsop (1995) have argued that the importance of questions is that:

- they can indicate areas of understanding and incomprehension;
- they can show the willingness of children to *seek* understanding;
- science itself is based on asking questions and seeking answers.

Yet, how often, do we give children the opportunity to ask questions themselves? One simple strategy, often used effectively in sex education, but rarely extended to other areas of science, is to have a question box into which children can put their questions anonymously. Another useful technique, often used in primary schools, is to have a large outline figure on a notice board called 'Professor Question'. Children are encouraged to pin questions to the figure as and when they arise. Simply starting any topic, for instance, astronomy, with the request for children to write down ten questions about the proposed subject of study can provide a fascinating insight into children's curiosity.

Opportunities for more group work and discussion is one strategy which children themselves have identified as something that would improve their enjoyment of science (Piburn, 1993). Whilst science teaching is often dominated by exigencies of the moment and the demands of adjusting to an ever-changing National Curriculum, can we as teachers of science afford to neglect an examination of the range and success of our teaching strategies? I hope this article provides a few crumbs as food for thought. Like the addict who tries to give up smoking, offering a lesson with no practical work may be a testing and unnerving experience, but it is my belief that the long-term gains for the health of science education are well worth the short-term pain.

Acknowledgements

I would like to thank Dr Bob Fairbrother for introducing me to the false concept map, an anonymous New Zealand teacher for showing me the use of jumbled sentences and Justin Dillon for comments on an early draft of this article.

References

Adamzyk, P., Willson, M. and Williams, D. (1994) Concept mapping: a multi-level and multi-purpose tool. *School Science Review*, 76(275), 116–124.

Bruner, J. and Haste, H. (1987) *Making sense: the child's construction of the World*. London: Methuen.

Cooper, P. and McIntyre, D. (1996) *Effective teaching and learning: teachers' and students' perspectives*. Buckingham: Open University Press.

Duschl, R. A. (1990) *Restructuring science education*. New York: Teachers College Press.

Edwards, D. and Mercer, N. (1987) *Common knowledge: the development of understanding in the classroom*. London: Methuen.

Horton, R. (1967) African traditional thought and western science. *Africa*, 37.

HM Inspectors of Schools (1994) *Effective learning and teaching in Scottish secondary schools: the sciences*. Edinburgh: The Scottish Office Education Department.

Lemke, J. L. (1990) Talking science: language, learning and values. In *Language and educational process*, ed. Green, J. Norwood, New Jersey: Ablex Publishing.

Novak, J. D. and Gowin, D. B. (1984) *Learning how to learn*. Cambridge: Cambridge University Press.

OFSTED (Office for Standards in Education) (1995) *Science: a review of inspection findings 1993/94*. London: HMSO.

Osborne, J. F. (1993) Alternatives to practical work. *School Science Review*, 75(271), 117–123.

Piburn, M. D. (1993) If I were the teacher... qualitative study of attitude toward science. *Science Education*, 77(4), 393–406.

Rowe, M. B. (1974) Relation of wait-time and rewards to the development of language, logic and fate control: Part II – Rewards. *Journal of Research in Science Teaching*, 11(4), 291–308.

Sands, M. K. (1981) Group work in science: myth and reality. School Science Review, 62(221), 765–769.

Sizmur, S. (1994) Concept mapping, language and learning in the classroom. *School Science Review*, 76(274), 120–125.

Watts, M. and Alsop, S. (1995) Questioning and conceptual understanding: the quality of pupils' questions in science. *School Science Review*, 76(277), 91–95.

Analysis

The extract introduces a number of strategies for engaging pupils in science without the use of practical or investigative work. But what common skills are developed? Firstly, Osborne refers to group work for discussion. This allows pupils not only to engage with the content but also to operate as scientists where progress is made through discussion. The use of group work must also feed into the key skills programme of study via the 'working with others' strand.

Secondly, Osborne introduces discussion of instances/misconceptions. Again this is not too far removed, conceptually, from investigation; the difference being that the question under investigation is resolved by discourse, by logic, by the use of the philosophy of science.

Concept maps are also a vehicle for discussion and group work which again draws on key skills and a more philosophical approach. Such approaches, which may appeal to many pupils, should not be underestimated and despite our support for investigative work, variety is vital for pupil engagement.

Personal response

Think back to your own time in school, at Key Stages 3 and 4. What guidance did you receive regarding investigative work?

What guidance did you receive at A-level and as an undergraduate?

Think of when you have observed investigative work in school or college. What guidance did the pupils receive?

Practical implications and activities

1. With a colleague, design a brief and appropriate prompt sheets for a Key Stage 3 investigation and discuss the outcome with your school based mentor.

- After discussion with your mentor and possible revision, arrange to carry out the investigation with a class.

- Assess each pupil against the National Curriculum level descriptors before reviewing a sample with your mentor. Following the discussion, do you need to revise your levels before returning the scripts to the pupils?

2. With a colleague, design a self-assessment sheet for Levels 2 to 5. Discuss your results with your school-based mentor.

Further reading

Gott, R. and Duggan, S. (1995) *Investigative Work in the Science Curriculum*. Buckingham: Open University Press.

NIAS (1998) *The New Sc1 Book. Experimental and Investigative Science*. Northamptonshire: NIAS.

Sci-Journal http://www.sci-journal.org/index.php?c_check=1 (accessed 27 January 2006)

6 Health and safety in the science laboratory

By the end of this chapter you will have considered and reflected upon:

- **what** is the likelihood of a serious accident happening in the school laboratory;
- **why** risk assessments are an essential part of lesson planning;
- **how** safety can be an integral part of teaching and learning in science.

Linking your learning
Achieving QTS Reflective Reader: Secondary Professional Studies. Hoult, S. (2005)
Chapter 4.

Roden, J. (2005) *Achieving QTS Reflective Reader: Primary Science.* Chapters 3 and
4. Exeter: Learning Matters.

Professional Standards for QTS
1.8, 2.1, 2.2, 2.7, 3.1.3, 3.3.2, 3.3.2d, 3.3.8, 3.3.9

Introduction

The issue of safety is not just a consideration or merely an important issue to take into consideration when planning a lesson; it is probably **the** most important factor in science, or any other subject, which overrides all others. In the words of Wellington (2000, p. 115), 'If it is unsafe or unhealthy in any way then do not do it.' However, many activities that, in their original form, might prove to be dangerous could, with relatively minor modification, be made safe. For example, the extraction of chlorophyll from leaves with ethanol heated in a Bunsen flame would be so unsafe as to render it unusable, even as a teacher demonstration, while it could be used as a practical activity with a suitable class if the source of heat were to be hot water. This raises an important issue, in that it is not only the inanimate components of a lesson that need to be taken into consideration but also the organic ones, in the shape of the class being taught. What might be acceptable for a small, co-operative, high-achieving Year 11 class may not be suitable for younger, larger or less well-behaved groups.

This chapter is intended to serve as an introduction to the issue of health and safety, to raise an awareness of some of the important factors. It cannot serve as a definitive guide and there are numerous detailed sources of information in the form of documents, ICT resources and books that would be classed as essential reading, some of which are listed at the end of this chapter.

What

In the minds of many, school science laboratories may appear dangerous places. However, despite these fears, in comparison with the seemingly 'safe' areas of a school, the laboratory is a far less common location for serious accidents than one might imagine, as may be seen in Table 6.1.

Table 6.1 Major accidents to pupils in schools (%)

Sports activities	38.5
Gymnasium	27.0
Playground	12.1
Corridors, stairs and cloakrooms	7.3
Classrooms	7.1
Extramural activities	1.5
Toilets	1.3
Science laboratories	0.9
Design and technology	0.7
Other	3.7

(Source: Health and Safety Executive Statistics for 1991/1992)

Even though school science is a considerably safer activity than many others, this should not be a cause for complacency and many accidents could have been prevented. Although rather dated, Tawney's report (1981) highlights that chemicals and their use, are to be the source of most school laboratory accidents (see Table 6.2).

Table 6.2 Most common school laboratory accidents (%)

Chemicals in the eye	23
Chemicals on the skin	21
Cuts	20
Burns and scalds	15
Falling, slipping, etc.	7
Chemicals in the mouth	4
Inhalation	4
Animal bites	3
Explosions	2
Fainting	2
Electric shocks	1

Personal response

Consider your own experience as a science learner, both in school and higher education. Can you think of activities or practices that you carried out which, upon reflection, you may not wish to use with your own classes?

Practical implications and activities

1. While on a school placement, find out where the reported accidents are recorded in order to see if the data listed above agree with the figures for your school.

2. Consider the following activities and try to decide if the statement is true or false:

a) The use of human saliva for enzyme experiments is banned in schools.
b) Because of the possibility of severe allergic reactions, measuring of the energy available from a burning peanut is now banned.
c) Pond dipping is now inadvisable because of the risk of catching Weil's disease.
d) The high voltages produced by a van de Graaff generator could be responsible for a fatal shock and therefore its use is banned.
e) You are not permitted to use an air gun in school for momentum and energy conservation experiments.

Why

Under the Management of Health and Safety at Work Regulations of 1992 (HSW Act), it is the employer's responsibility to ensure effective measures in planning, organisation, control and review of safety in order to provide a safe working environment for their employees. Strange as it may seem, these regulations do not extend to pupils but they do indicate the more general duty of care for non-employees. Although the neglect of safety precautions is a criminal offence, in the 21 years following the introduction of the HSW Act in 1975 there were only two successful prosecutions of science teachers and these were both as a result of a blatant disregard of safety precautions and not a minor misjudgement (ASE, 1996).

A number of regulations have been enacted under the umbrella of the HSW Act but these are three of the more important ones for the science teacher:

- The Control of Substances Hazardous to Health (COSHH), which focuses upon corrosive, harmful, irritant and toxic substance as well as harmful micro-organisms and dust.
- The Management of Health and Safety at Work Regulations, which extends the risk assessment principles in the COSHH regulations to all hazards.
- The Provision and Use of Work Equipment Regulations, which are intended to ensure that equipment is constructed safely and is maintained satisfactorily.

Personal response

Consider additional areas of science that you think should be covered by statutory safety requirements.

As with many aspects of the National Curriculum for Science, there is a statutory requirement within the area focusing upon general teaching requirements that pupils should be taught:

a) about hazards, risks and risk control;
b) to recognise hazards, assess consequent risks and take steps to control the risks to themselves and others;
c) to use information to assess the immediate and cumulative risks;

d) to manage their environment to ensure the health and safety of themselves and others;

e) to explain the steps they take to control risks.

(DfEE, 1999, p. 71)

Practical implications and activities

Consult a copy of the National Curriculum for Science (an on-line version may be found at: www.nc.uk.net) to find references to other requirements for the teaching of health and safety.

How

Before completing this section, refer to your responses to activity 1 at the end of the 'What' section of this chapter. In reality, there are few activities that are banned in schools at a national level although they may be at a local or school level, in which case an employee must follow the ruling of his or her employer.

The task of carrying out a risk assessment may be delegated to an employee. However, as stated earlier, the responsibility still remains with the employer to ensure that such assessments are carried out before any hazardous activity takes place or hazardous chemicals and micro-organisms are used. It is the responsibility of the employer to check that these delegated tasks competently.

Before you read the extract, read:

• Wellington, J. (2000) *Teaching and Learning Secondary Science* (pages 115–117). London: Routledge.

Extract: Borrows, P. (1998) Safety in science education, in Ratcliffe, M. *ASE Guide to Secondary Science Education*. Hatfield: The Association for Science Education. Pages 184–185.

Risk assessment

The key to managing safety in school science – and, indeed, elsewhere – is risk assessment. In practice, science teachers have been carrying out risk assessment since long before the phrase was invented.

A *hazard* is anything with the potential to cause harm. Hazards will therefore include many chemicals, electricity at high voltages and such activities as carrying a tray of microscopes up and down stairs. In the particular case of chemicals, the hazard is an intrinsic property of the chemical.

Risk is the probability that harm will actually be caused by the hazard. There are two elements to risk:

• How likely is it that something will go wrong?
• How serious would it be if something did go wrong?

Risk assessment involves answering these two questions and then deciding what control measures, if any, are necessary to reduce the risk. Risk assessment is the employer's responsibility and it must be carried out before a hazardous activity is undertaken. This might seem a daunting task given the large number of schools and the relative freedom for teachers within those schools to plan how they will teach the National Curriculum. Soon after the COSHH Regulations were implemented, education employers were given guidance (HSC, 1989) about how this might be achieved:

> In order to help those undertaking these responsibilities, a number of general assessments have already been developed for most of the substances and experiments found in school science. Examples are included in the second edition of the Association for Science Education's (ASE's) Topics in Safety and the Hazards produced jointly by the Consortium of Local Education Authorities for the Provision of Science Services (CLEAPSS) and the Scottish Schools Equipment Research Centre (SSERC) ...

For science subjects, employers have the choice of

(a) adopting and if necessary adapting to particular circumstances such well researched and established general assessments for school science work ....

This approach was made more formal by inclusion in the Approved Code of Practice accompanying the Management of Health and Safety at Work Regulations:

Employers who control a number of similar workplaces containing similar activities may produce a basic 'model' risk assessment reflecting the core hazards and risks associated with these activities. 'Model' assessments may also be developed by trade associations, employers' bodies or other organisations concerned with a particular activity. Such 'model' assessments may be applied by employers or managers at each workplace, but only if they:

(a) satisfy themselves that the 'model' assessment is broadly appropriate to their type of work; and

(b) adapt the 'model' to the detail of their own actual work situations, including any extension necessary to cover hazards and risks not referred to in the 'model'.

Note that 'model', 'general' and 'generic' risk assessments mean the same thing – the terminology has changed over the years. Most education employers have followed this advice and adopted a number of standard safety texts as the basis for their model risk assessments. Here it will be assumed that this is the approach to be followed but if employers have adopted a different procedure then teachers and technicians are obliged to co-operate with it. Some employers, particularly small independent schools, do not make their procedure for risk assessment clear, or they attempt to pass the responsibility to the head of department. If they have not been given clear guidance, staff in such schools are advised to follow the procedures suggested here, but their employer still has legal responsibility and staff should inform their employer in writing that that is what they are doing.

Analysis

In the extract, the author identifies two components to a risk assessment.

- How likely is it that something will go wrong?
- How serious would it be if something did go wrong?

However, we would wish to add additional factors.

- A consideration of what the teacher would do if an accident were to happen and what advance preparations could be carried out to minimise the effect. For example, if a mercury thermometer were to be dropped on the floor and break, how might the spill be dealt with in order to reduce the amount of mercury vapour entering the atmosphere?
- Does the activity have a valid educational aim?
- Is there an alternative, safer activity that could enable the same educational aim to be achieved?

Although mechanistic, some teachers find it helpful to rate the original two possibilities highlighted in the extract on a scale of 1 to 5, so that something unlikely to happen would be rated as 1, while something highly likely would be rated as 5. Similarly, a trivial incident would be rated as 1 and something life-threatening as 5. Multiplying the two ratings would give an overall score out of a possible 25. The closer the overall score is to 25, the greater the risk and the more unwise it would be to carry out the activity.

For example, asking a Year 7 class to dissolve sodium chloride in a beaker of water might involve the risk of a pupil getting salt water into his or her eye or of breaking the beaker and cutting a finger. In such a case, the likelihood of something going wrong might be pretty high with an inexperienced class and a rating of 3 may be appropriate. The seriousness of a water splash would be negligible but a cut might be rated as 2. The combined score out of 25 would be $3 \times 2 = 6$, a relatively low score which would indicate that the activity should be safe to carry out. However, even with such activities, we should still strive to minimise the risk and substituting plastic beakers for glass ones and insisting that pupils wore safety spectacles would reduce the risk even further.

Referring to the experiment mentioned in the introduction, in which chlorophyll is extracted from leaves with ethanol heated by a naked Bunsen flame, the chance of something going wrong would be very high and a rating of 4 out of 5 appropriate. If the ethanol were to catch light then, while a resultant burn may not be life-threatening, it could be serious and given a rating of 4 out of 5. The combined score would be $4 \times 4 = 16$, a score high enough to render such an experiment unsuitable for even a demonstration. However, by replacing the Bunsen as a source of heat with hot water, the chance of the ethanol catching light would be reduced and the experiment could be considered suitable for an appropriate, well-monitored class.

Practical implications and activities

Refer to the five activities noted earlier in this chapter and, in consultation with your mentor, consider:
- What precautions you might take in order to minimise the chance of something going wrong?
- What you should do in the eventuality of an accident happening?

For a beginning teacher, or even an experienced one, it would be wise to make a record of risk assessments carried out in the lesson plan, scheme of work or worksheets. Some employers may have adopted a range of general or model risk assessments and these guidelines may form part of the department's policy documents. In such cases it is the employee's responsibility to ensure that the guidance is adhered to. However, on occasions the proposed activity involves a novel situation and in such circumstances the individual teacher would need to carry out a special risk assessment. For the beginning teacher it would be wise to consult his or her head of department for advice in such situations or if they are at all unclear as to what the employer's requirements are.

It is important that pupils are taken through the processes involved in assessing risks and this will not only fulfil the requirements of the National Curriculum but also prepare them for the hazards of home and work. To this end, CLEAPSS (2000) have produced pupil versions of teachers' safety sheets. In involving pupils in the process of risk assessment, particularly when planning their own investigations, they are able to contribute to their own safety. Having said that, such procedures do not absolve the teacher from his or her responsibility of ensuring that pupils' proposed activities are in accordance with the employers' risk assessments.

Further reading

ASE (1988) *Topics in Safety*. Hatfield: ASE.

ASE (1996) *Safeguards in the School Laboratory*. Hatfield: ASE.

ASE (1998) *Safety Reprints*. Hatfield: ASE.

ASE (1999) *Safe and Exciting Science*. Hatfield: ASE.

Borrows, P. (1998) 'Safety in Science Education', in Ratcliffe, M. *ASE Guide to Secondary Science Education*. Hatfield: The Association for Science Education.

CLEAPSS (2000) *Student Safety Sheets*. CLEAPSS: Brunel University.

CLEAPSS (2002) *Science Publications CD ROM*. CLEAPSS: Brunel University.

DfEE (1996) *Safety in Science Education*. Norwich: HMSO.

Everett, D. and Jenkins, E. (1990) *A Safety Handbook for Science Teachers*. London: John Murray.

HMSO (1985) *Microbiology: An HMI guide for schools and non-advanced further education*. London: HMSO.

Royal Society of Chemistry (2005) 'Surely That's Banned? A report for the Royal Society of Chemistry on chemicals and procedures thought to be banned from use in schools'. http://www.rsc.org

Scottish Schools Science Equipment Research Centre (1981) *Hazardous Chemicals: A manual for schools and colleges*. Edinburgh: Oliver and Boyd.

7 The purpose of practical work

By the end of this chapter you will have considered and reflected upon:

- **why** practical work is important in science;
- **what** types of practical work exists;
- **how** should practical work be organised.

Linking your learning
Before reading this chapter, read Chapter 1, 'Planning for effective learning in science'; Chapter 5, 'Planning and assessing investigations in science'; Chapter 6, 'Health and safety in the science laboratory'.

Professional Standards for QTS
2.1, 2.1c, 2.1d, 3.1.3, 3.3.2, 3.3.2c, 3.3.2d, 3.3.8

Introduction

Sine experimentia nihil sufficienter sciri protest.

('Without experiments nothing can be adequately known.')
(Engraving over the doorway of the Daubeny building, Oxford, used for some time as the site of some of the earliest science teaching in the University.)

Although today we may view practical work as an essential component of scientific study, this has not always been the case. For example, the Thompson Report of 1918 criticised practical work as wasteful of time and advocated teacher demonstrations as a more cost-effective approach. Some 20 years later, the Spens Report (1938) was reiterating this view and by 1946 Cunningham's review of evaluations of the respective merits of individual practical work as opposed to teacher demonstrations only served to muddy the waters by revealing no decisive benefit either way.

However, by the 1960s and via the generous funding of the Nuffield Foundation, we find a heuristic (discovery learning) approach being advocated. In the introduction to the then new Nuffield Chemistry course (1966) the aim of the scheme is stated to be:

To awaken the spirit of investigation and to develop disciplined investigative thinking.

Although the aim may have been admirable, the reality was that some of the experiments and pieces of apparatus were so contrived and controlled that they only differed from the illustrative experiments of the previous century in that the pupils were not told in advance what law or principle they were attempting to verify. In many respects the scheme was more one of 'right answerism' rather than one of genuine discovery. Even Her Majesty's Inspectorate (HMI, 1979) was critical of such an approach and advocated more teacher demonstrations and less Nuffield-style practicals.

Shortly after, the tide began to turn and by 1982 the Department for Education and Science (DES) were stating that:

> Designing investigations is, therefore, an important activity although it seems to be neglected.

The time was ripe then for a different approach to practical work in schools and, in an attempt to emulate similar American schemes, Peter Screen (1986) launched his Warwick Process Science, in which the importance of observing, classifying, inferring, interpreting and hypothesising were paramount, with scientific content subservient. Screen argued that a knowledge-led curriculum has little relevance but that there are:

> qualities of science education which might be termed primary or generic qualities which will be of value when the facts are out of date or forgotten.

This is a view supported by the DES (1985) policy, in which it states that:

> Courses provided should … give pupils opportunities to … suggest and carry out experiments … handle equipment safely … use their knowledge in conducting investigations.

Perhaps as a result of schemes such as those advocated by Screen (1986) or the introduction of a National Curriculum for science, by 1989 the DES was reporting a higher success rate for investigative problems than for some other forms of assessment.

Why

With the cost of equipping and servicing a typical school laboratory being on a par with the purchase and maintenance of a small house, it does not seem unreasonable to ask educators to make a hard-headed evaluation of the justification of such expense. There are, in all probability, countless science teachers who have viewed practical work as a generally beneficial activity, not questioning its purpose or educational value, and this state of affairs is summarised by Hodson (1990) as:

> teachers use it [practical work] unthinkingly. Not because they are unthinking people, but because they have been subject to the powerful, myth-making rhetoric of the profession that sees hands-on practical work as the universal panacea, the educational solution to all learning problems.

So why do we place such emphasis upon practical work – what is there about this aspect of science teaching that justifies schools spending thousands of pounds upon its pursuit? In the extract below, Wellington considers some of the arguments posed for doing practical work in science lessons.

Extract: Wellington, J. (2000) *Teaching and Learning Secondary Science.* **Routledge. Pages 145–147.**

Why do practical work in science lessons?

An enormous amount of time and money is invested in making practical work an element of secondary school science. Schools employ lab technicians, consume consumables of all kinds and invest large sums in pieces of apparatus that most pupils have never seen elsewhere and are never likely to encounter again after school. In the current era of local management and devolved budgets, it is inevitable that the traditional expense of practical work will be questioned by someone running the school. Science teachers need to be able to justify the time and money spent on practical work not only for this reason, but also in order to answer the two further questions of '*what?*' and '*how?*'

In 1963, Kerr organised a survey of 701 science teachers from 151 schools in order to find out why they did practical work in school science. He suggested ten aims or purposes which those in the survey were asked to rank for importance in relation to three different age ranges: lower secondary, upper secondary and 'sixth form'. The aims presented to teachers are shown in Table 7.1.

Table 7.1 Ten possible aims of practical work

---

1 To encourage accurate observation and careful recording.
2 To promote simple, common-sense, scientific methods of thought.
3 To develop manipulative skills.
4 To give training in problem-solving.
5 To fit the requirements of practical examinations.
6 To elucidate the theoretical work so as to aid comprehension.
7 To verify facts and principles already taught.
8 To be an integral part of the process of finding facts by investigation and arriving at principles.
9 To arouse and maintain interest in the subject.
10 To make biological, chemical and physical phenomena more real through actual experience.

Source: Used by Kerr, 1963.

It is interesting to note that those aims are still largely relevant today, four decades on. Before reading further, consider each of those aims carefully and rank them for yourself for different ages of pupils. Jot down your own ranking for: years 7, 8 and 9; years 10 and 11; years 12 and 13 (the 'sixth form').

The full analysis of results is well worth reading in full (Kerr, 1963). Here is my own potted summary of the responses:

- there was a change in emphasis in practical work as pupils move through the secondary school, for example, away from arousing interest towards careful recording;

- however, observation and scientific thinking were ranked highly throughout;
- aim 9 was highest for years 7–9;
- aim 1 was highest for years 12–13.

Taking all teachers and all age groups into account, the overall ranking of aims was: 1 (first), 2 and 8 (joint second), 6, 10, 9, 7, 3, 4, 5 (last). How do these compare with your own ranking?

The role and potential of practical work

The place of practical work in science *needs* to be justified; fortunately, there are many useful discussions which help by giving us a framework for practical work by outlining its purpose and potential. These can be summarised only briefly here.

Woolnough and Allsop (1985), in an excellent discussion on practical science, suggest that in the past four types of aim have been given by teachers and curriculum developers for small-group practicals:

1 motivational, i.e. that practical science can motivate and interest pupils (cf. Kerr 1963);
2 the development of experimental skills and techniques, such as observation, measurement, handling apparatus, etc.;
3 simulating the work of a real scientist – 'being a real scientist for the day' (a phrase from the early Nuffield days);
4 supporting theory, i.e. using practical to 'discover', elucidate or illuminate theory; and improving retention in line with the other catch-phrase of practical work: 'I hear and I forget, I see and I remember, I do and I understand.'

Analysis

The four reasons given for carrying out practical work, taken at face value, may seem justifiable but in reality may not always reflect the rhetoric.

1. Motivation is an affective intangible, that is difficult to quantify, while at the same time being glaringly obvious to all but the most insensitive, which teachers ignore at their peril. Teachers may impose an extrinsic motivational force upon their pupils but the effect is likely to be short-lived and, if it is to have more than a transient nature, it requires the awakening in the pupil of an intrinsic form. As Woolnough (1991) writes:

> *Students may fail not because they cannot but because they do not want to. A student who wants to succeed on a scientific task, and has the self-confidence to tackle it, may reveal ways of working and a grasp of the underlying theory which was unexpected.*

How often have you heard a science teacher being asked, 'Can't we do practical today, sir/miss?' and this, on the surface, appears to reflect an eagerness to be engaged in a more physically active form of study. Denny and Chennell (1986), though, report studies which reveal that, although the majority of pupils may be favourably disposed towards practical activities, there is a disturbing, and all too common, undercurrent of feeling that practical activity is viewed merely as a 'less boring' alternative to other classroom activities.

As Solomon (1980) writes, pupils enter secondary school:

> *all agog to 'do experiments', to touch and use the strange new instruments and per-*
> *form exciting tricks with them. To put it at its lowest level, this is a wonderful op-*
> *portunity for new play.*

Is it that these pupils, lacking the immediate pressure of public examinations, carry out fairly open-ended and personal investigations? All too often, this is replaced for older pupils by having to carry out directed experiments in order to illustrate an important fact or concept that does not emanate from within the pupil but is examination specifi-cation-inspired. At best, pupils may be urged to 'discover' a law or predetermined fact, only to have their findings devalued when they are given the 'right' answer by the teacher. Does this in some way explain a reported decline in enthusiasm for practical work as pupils grow older (Hodson, 1990)?

2. In research intended to contrast the effectiveness of differing laboratory experiences in science teaching, the overwhelming evidence was, not surprisingly, found to be that pupils with 'hands-on' practical experience developed far greater manipulative skills than those deprived of such experiences. It may be that such skills are important for and transferable to everyday life experiences, but Adey (1988) chronicles, what many teachers would attest to, the inability of pupils to transfer concepts learnt in one situa-tion to more diverse fields. Within secondary science it is unlikely that anything other than those skills of a relatively trivial nature are essential and indeed most higher-order skills are, in all probability, demonstrated or simulated. Even if such manual skills are of importance, we, as science teachers, have historically been singularly inept at their instruction. A survey carried out by the Assessment of Performance Unit (APU, 1989) revealed that more than 60 per cent of the 13-year-old population were unable to correctly read such common laboratory instruments as a force meter or measuring cylinder.

3. The aura of a scientist has been one of a person who is not only able to approach problems in an open-minded and value-free manner but also suspends judgement until all the facts are known and cross-checked. Not only have we been encouraged to accept this as the 'scientific shop front' but also that these qualities are indeed ones that we would encourage our pupils to emulate. Kuhn (1963) argued that any pupil capable of such an approach would be the exception rather than the rule and this view resonates with that of Driver (1983), who argues that 'pupils, like scientists, view the world through spectacles of their own preconceptions'. Mahoney (1979) highlights the illogical nature of scientists who are not above bias in the selection of which data to promote or suppress.

Taking an interpersonal stance, one is tempted to question the wisdom of portraying science as impersonal and dispassionate. Perhaps this view may have played some part in dissuading teenagers from following the path of physical science instead of opting for the more affective face of the social sciences. If the stereotypical scientist is but a myth of our own creation, as Gaud (1982) argues:

> *teaching that scientists posses these characteristics is bad enough, but it is abhor-rent that science educators should actually attempt to mould children in the same false image.*

4. It is certainly true that to handle and observe certain phenomena is the only way to gain an understanding of them. One may read about the colour of copper sulphate crystals, repulsion between magnets or the spontaneous combustion of a stick of phos-phorus, but to experience them first-hand creates a far deeper understanding. How many of us, old enough to have been part of a less safety-conscious era, can forget the wonder of chasing an almost magical silver pool of mercury along the bench with a finger or forget the unmistakable stench of a tube of illicitly prepared hydrogen sulphide? Woolnough and Allsop (1985) described this as getting a 'feel for the phenomena'. On occasions though, the property witnessed is not the one that the teacher intended. The pupil may well have noticed some apparently trivial (in the eyes of the teacher) but no less valid factor during the practical experience and this may serve not to give him or her a deeper understanding but merely to confuse, and this is termed by Hodson (1992) as 'pedagogic noise'. Rather than being useful in the develop-ment of new concepts, much practical activity could be providing a vast amount of experimental clutter. In essence, it may be that our pupils are not processing the infor-mation and forming their own internal framework but that they are either forming a different one to that intended or reinforcing existing misconceptions.

Personal response

Consider the 10 possible aims for practical work in the extract. What additional aims would you choose to add to the list?

Practical implications and activities

Consult a scheme of work used in one of your placement schools. Read through the scheme and, using Kerr's 10 aims for practical work, assess how many of the aims are being addressed. If any of the aims are omitted, consider if it/they should have been included and, if so, how could the scheme be modified to address all of them. Are there occasions when a practical activity could be carried out but you would consider it inadvisable to do so? Discuss your ideas with a colleague.

What

Wellington (2000) classes practical work under six general headings. To this list, could be added Internet-supported activities and thought experiments.

Demonstrations

With a push for more investigative work in science, teacher demonstrations may not be as commonly presented as in earlier years. However, there are many reasons for carrying out demonstrations, for example:

- the experiment is potentially dangerous in the hands of a pupil (or, as in the case where radioactive sources are used, illegal);
- the apparatus used is either expensive or in short supply;
- the experiment demands skills beyond those of the pupils;
- the experiment would be too time consuming for a class activity;
- there is the facility to present the concept with greater clarity;
- the teacher wishes to demonstrate a skill to be used later by the class.

There is a valuable place in science teaching for a good demonstration which can offer the opportunity to provide the class with a large-scale, memorable and entertaining experience that has great impact.

Class experiments

With whole-class practicals, in addition to presenting pupils with the opportunity to enhance their practical skills, they also have first-hand experience of the phenomena; they are, hopefully, motivated by the experience, may be challenged cognitively by their observations and generate data for further discussion and analysis. One other important factor, missing from these examples, is that pupils develop skills of working in small groups and through communicating with each other have the opportunity to test their ideas on others, coupled with developing their thinking through challenging each other's ideas. Group size is an important issue: too large and some pupils may be left uninvolved on the sidelines, too small and there is not the opportunity for productive group discussions.

Circus activities

For situations where the apparatus is in short supply or a range of activities would be desirable, a 'circus' approach is useful. In the case of, for example, a series of energy transformation activities, there could be a range of apparatus distributed around the room and the pupils could experience each in rapid succession.

Simulation and role play

With many aspects of science, the 'real thing' would be impossible to experience, for example sheer size in the case of tectonic plate movement and planetary motion is impractical to experience in any way other than modelling or simulation. Referring to radioactivity once more, while a demonstration or a video recording is the only legal option with real sources, it is possible for pupils to model radioactive decay and get a feel for half-life by tracking the decay of the foam on the top of beer or shandy or of the height of a column of viscous liquid flowing out of a modified burette.

Allied to the idea of simulating a process via a real or virtual model is that of the pupils themselves becoming active components in the model through role play. When dealing with unseen particles at an atomic or molecular level, it may be difficult for many pupils to understand the idea of particle motion in solids, liquids and gases and the processes involved in changing from one state to another. Having a class acting out the concepts can give many, particularly the kinaesthetic learners, a better understanding of what is involved in something which, in reality, is the model that scientists have generated to enable them to deal with the ideas; strangely enough, a model to help children understand a more sophisticated model!

Investigations

As covered in more detail in Chapter 5, it would appear that the term 'investigation' means different things to different people. However, we are of the belief that investigations should be at the heart of practical work in science and may range in length from part of a lesson to something that lasts several weeks, they could be carried out by individuals or within groups, in the classroom, at home or, via the Internet, in collaboration with children from different schools or countries. The best investigations are those which have relevance for the pupils and should start with a question that is applicable to their everyday lives. It is not uncommon for teachers to ask their pupils, after being introduced to the problem, to produce a plan to be executed. It could be argued, though, that this approach does not mirror that of 'real' scientists who are likely to react to issues arising as they proceed and modify their approach accordingly.

Problem-solving activities

Using a problem from everyday life, with the need for a solution, gives this approach more relevance to pupils. In particular, a more technologically based investigation can focus pupils' attention to a greater extent than a more theoretical approach used in some investigations. For example, 'finding the best temperature at which to ferment alcohol with yeast' or 'the best temperature to use when washing clothes with a biological washing powder' should result in a single recommendation as opposed to the more theoretical approach involved in involving essentially the same science when 'investigating the effect of temperature on enzymes'. Both approaches, we would argue, involve similar strategies for the pupils in that they are given a problem to solve which they are encouraged to place in a scientific context. The pupils need to consider a series of ideas that could be tested and, from a range of approaches, select the optimum one. A problem-solving activity, however, would usually involve arriving at a solution or the production of an artefact. With this approach, there is no one correct answer, merely a range of answers to be evaluated.

Internet supported activities

In some cases, although the real apparatus may be neither expensive nor dangerous, the advantage of an Internet-based simulation is that there is no mad scramble for the equipment, pupils can work at their own rate and the experiment 'always works'. An example here would be the construction of a simple electric motor which, although a fun and productive activity, can be extremely time-consuming and problematic. In addition, some activities may be unethical in reality. Take, for example, the relationship between the fertility/population size of birds of prey and the use of pesticides. Historical data can be obtained on bird populations whilst pesticide production can be found on other sites and relationships between the two investigated. Similarly, by accessing power station, environmental agency and meteorological websites, connections can be investigated, between variables such as power station output, air temperature, wind direction and air quality.

Though experiments

Thought experiments are devices of the imagination used to investigate the nature of things. Examples of well-known thought experiments are Schrödinger's cat, Newton's bucket and the Chinese room. To gain a better understanding of a thought experiment, consider Galileo's experiment in which he supposedly dropped balls from the tower of Pisa. The result holds for objects dropped in a vacuum but Italy was not in a vacuum when the experiment supposedly was carried out. Ireson (2005) contends that it is unlikely that Galileo actually carried out the experiment, rather that he carried out the following simple thought experiment:

The rate of falling of a heavy ball is H.

The rate of falling of a light ball is L.

If a heavy ball falls faster then $H > L$.

Therefore the two together must fall faster than the heavy ball alone, since $(H + L) > H$

But the two balls must fall slower than the heavy ball alone since the lighter ball will drag the heavy ball and this can be notated as $(H + L) < H$

The only way this can be true is if $H = L$

One might be tempted to consider this approach to be one for the most able, but is it not what we ask of our pupils when planning any investigation in which, although not expressed in such eloquent terms as those used by Schrödinger or Newton, we require children to adopt a theoretical approach to a problem, set up a 'what if' statement and consider what is predicted to happen 'because'? Admittedly though, we do not usually ask our pupils to complete the entire investigation as a theoretical exercise but they are, at least, expected to produce a testable hypothesis.

Personal response

Think back to your time either at school/college or university. What sort of practical activity did you experience?

Practical implications and activities

Refer to the scheme of work used in your placement school that you have or are just about to use. Which of the given types of practical work are included?

How

Taking practical work as a whole, there are some generic considerations which we would seek to address first. Drawing upon the advice of Wellington (2000), some general rules for all practical activities would include the following:

- The activity must be safe (see Chapter 6) and any precautions that could be taken must be, whether for pupils or teachers; if teachers do not model good practice then how can they expect their pupils to do so?
- If you have not carried out the experiment before then you must try it out in advance and this applies to demonstrations and circus activities as well as more regular class experiments.
- Order apparatus, support or facilities well in advance.
- Consider movement around the room, especially for the distribution of apparatus. Try to avoid excessive movement and spread available apparatus out to avoid congestion.
- Give clear instructions, appropriate for the individuals; some may require verbal instructions, some demonstrations, some pictorial instructions and some written ones or a combination of all methods. Check that the pupils understand the instructions; just because you tell them does not mean that they either understand or remember.
- Make a show of counting equipment out and checking it back in. Some pieces of equipment have a tendency to 'disappear' if not carefully monitored.

Pupils are more than likely to arrive with preconceptions of how science works and it is these preconceptions that determine how any new information is interpreted. Your task then is two-fold. First, you have to tease out from the pupils what preconceptions they are bringing to the lesson, and second, you have to help them modify these ideas through discussion, aided by input from practical work, so that new ways of thinking are established that are acceptable to the scientific community.

Personal response

Consult the advice above for those using the Internet to support their science teaching. Are the points significantly different to those applying to more traditional practical activities? How could you modify the advice given here to make it more generally applicable to other practical experiences?

Practical implications and activities

- With demonstrations, it is helpful to have a worksheet available for the class to focus on. For a demonstration you are planning to carry out in the near future, construct a differentiated worksheet for the class to complete.
- Discuss your worksheet with your mentor well before the lesson and, if necessary, modify it before using it with the class.
- Carry out the demonstration and, taking your mentor's advice on its success, consider how you might modify the worksheet for use in the future.

Further reading

Gott, R. and Duggan, S. (1995) *Investigative Work in the Science Curriculum*. Buckingham: Open University Press.

McDuell, B. (2000) *Teaching Secondary Chemistry*. London: John Murray.

Reiss, M. (1999) *Teaching Secondary Biology*. London: John Murray.

Royal Society of Chemistry (2000) *Classic Chemistry Experiments*. London: RSC.

Sang, D. (2000) *Teaching Secondary Physics*. London: John Murray.

Sang, D. and Wood-Robinson, V. (2002) *Teaching Secondary Scientific Enquiry*. London: John Murray.

Woolnough, B. and Allsopp, T. (1985) *Practical Work in Science*. Cambridge: Cambridge University Press.

8 The nature of science

By the end of this chapter you should have considered and reflected upon:

- **why** the nature of science is important for learning and teaching;
- **what** your view of the nature of science is;
- **how** you might develop strategies to support pupils' understanding of the nature of science.

Linking your learning
Monk, M. and Dillan, J. (2000) The Nature of Scientific Knowledge, in Monk, M. and Osborne, J. *Good Practice in Science Teaching*. Buckingham: Open University Press.

Professional Standards for QTS
1.8, 2.1, 2.1c, 3.1.3, 3.3.2, 3.3.2c, 3.3.2d

Introduction

The importance of the nature of science is stressed in the National Curriculum for England and Wales (DfEE, 1999) at both Key Stages 3 and 4. At Key Stage 3, the National Curriculum states that pupils should be taught:

a) about the interplay between empirical questions, evidence and scientific explanations using historical and contemporary examples (for example, Lavoisier's work on burning, the possible causes of global warming);

b) that it is important to test explanations by using them to make predictions and by seeing if evidence matches the predictions;

c) about the ways in which scientists work today and how they worked in the past, including the roles of experimentation, evidence and creative thought in the development of scientific ideas.

However, from 2006, at Key Stage 4, the new programme of study (QCA, 2006), under the heading of 'How science works', extends this to include the requirement that pupils should be taught:

1c how explanations of many phenomena can be developed using scientific theories, models and ideas;

1d that there are some questions that science cannot currently answer, and some that science cannot address;

4a about the use of contemporary scientific and technological developments and their benefits, drawbacks and risks;

4b to consider how and why decisions about science and technology are made, including those that raise ethical issues, and about the social, economic and environmental effects of such decisions;

4c how uncertainties in scientific knowledge and scientific ideas change over time and about the role of the scientific community in validating these changes.

Similar, although not identical, requirements are to be found in the ACCAC publication (2000), *Science in the National Curriculum in Wales.*

In this chapter you will be encouraged to consider why the nature of science should be part of the curriculum. You will then be encouraged to assess what your own view of what the nature of science is. Finally, you will be guided towards developing your own strategy for embedding the nature of science in your own teaching.

Why

Before you read this extract, read:

- the NESTA-Futurelab 'Literature Review in Science Education and the Role of ICT', available at: www.nestafuturelab.org/research/lit.reviews.htm.

Extract: Brickhouse, Zoubeida, Dagher, Shipman and Letts (2000) in Miller, Leach and Osborne (eds) *Improving Science Education*, Open University Press. Pages 11–13.

Science educators have argued for decades that the science curriculum must address not only learning science, but also learning about the nature of science (Matthews, 1994). In other words, it is insufficient to know specific theories of science and not know how knowledge claims are justified, what counts as evidence, or how theory and evidence interact.

Driver et al. (1996) identify five rationales for teaching about the nature of science. These are:

- A utilitarian argument: 'an understanding of science is necessary if people are to make sense of the science and manage the technological objects and processes they encounter in everyday life'.
- A democratic argument: 'an understanding of the nature of science is necessary if people are to make sense of socioscientific issues and participate in the decision-making process'.
- A cultural argument: 'an understanding of the nature of science is necessary in order to appreciate science as a major element of contemporary culture'.
- A moral argument: 'an understanding of the nature of science can help develop awareness of the nature of science, and in particular the norms of the scientific community, embodying moral commitments that are of general value'.
- A science learning argument: 'an understanding of the nature of science supports successful learning of science content'.

Arguments like these have made the nature of science part of curriculum debates across the globe. In England and Wales, the nature of science is incorporated into the National Curriculum (NC) (Driver et al., 1996). The nature of science is a significant part of the US National Science Education Standards (NRC, 1995) and appears as part of many state standards documents (e.g. in Delaware).

We wonder, however, if it is possible to talk meaningfully about a 'universal nature' of science. Some researchers have argued that learning about the nature of science is invariant to content understanding. For example, Kuhn et al. (1988) investigated the ability of young children to make distinctions between theory and evidence. They conclude that the ability to coordinate theory and evidence is a general ability rather than a domain-specific one. However, the contexts for the questions the researchers asked were not embedded in the conceptual content of science. Instead, the 'theories' they used are more like people's everyday theories – for example, what kind of food makes people more likely to catch a cold? Since these kinds of theory are familiar and require little understanding of scientific theories, it is not surprising that understanding content had little influence on the responses to the reasoning questions.

Some research makes generalisations about what students understand about the nature of science without considering the possibility of how this might vary from one scientific domain to the next. In some cases, the research is large-scale in nature and utilises surveys to assess general principles about the nature of science. Whereas Driver et al. (1996) designed problems that are embedded in school science content, the conclusions that are drawn are generalised to all science content. In other cases, the research is an assessment of a particular classroom intervention, yet neither the intervention nor the assessment takes into account the role of science content (Abd-El-Khalick et al., 1998). Finally, some researchers implement interventions that are based in specific-subject matter, yet assess student learning without regard for student understanding of subject matter, and generalise to all science content (Carey et al., 1989; Roth and Lucas, 1997).

Over a decade ago Millar and Driver (1987) argued that how students actually used science process skills was dependent on their understanding of science content. A similar rationale may well be appropriately applied to teaching about the nature of science. Samarapungavan (1992) has argued that changes in children's reasoning on theory-choice tasks can be accounted for by changes in their understanding of the underlying scientific concepts. While the recent work of Driver et al. (1996) does not directly address this possibility, their data are consistent with the idea that students' warrants for belief in scientific ideas and their abilities to coordinate theory and evidence vary somewhat with content. For example, they found that students talked differently about evidence and explanation when given a story about rusting than they did when given a story about balloons filled with air.

Finally, recent scholarship questions the validity of constructing meta-narratives of science (Gallison and Stump, 1996; Stanley and Brickhouse, in press). General description of science, intended to apply to all the practices of the sciences, may be for the most part false or misleading. Science studies increasingly emphasise the local character of the sciences and the diversity of practices that are carried out under the name of science. For example, Hacking (1996) described different styles of reasoning and how they are a manifest part of the different sciences. Similarly, factors that drive research in one area may not be significant in another. For example, while theoretical development may be the motivation for scientific inquiry in some areas, in other areas technological advancement or the solution of practical difficulties may be more important.

Analysis

As seen above, a study of the nature of science is of long-standing international importance. The five rationales identified by Driver et al. (1996) are strong arguments for the inclusion of a study of the nature of science in any curriculum and, as such, are reflected in the National Curriculum for England and Wales (DfEE, 1999) and the US National Science Education Standards (NCR, 1995).

Whilst we would agree that the nature of science should form part of any school-based science curriculum, we would also argue that for anyone preparing to teach secondary science they should undertake an in-depth study of the nature of science. An important factor from this extract is that learning and teaching about the nature of science draws on more than just 'scientific knowledge'.

Personal response

Consider your own experience as a science learner. To what degree was the nature of science dealt with in your science lessons? Give two examples and discuss these with a colleague.

Practical implications and activities

Using information in the extract as a prompt, discuss with a peer why you believe that the nature of science is important for learning and teaching science.

What

We have seen some of the rationale given for why teaching about the nature of science is important. In this section, you will be asked to consider your own view of the nature of science.

The following extract is taken from an article by Nott and Wellington in which they encouraged science teachers to explore their own understanding of the nature of science. Many of the terms used may be unfamiliar. In fact, many of these are problematic and a matter of debate; the following are those given by Nott and Wellington.

Extract: Nott, M. and Wellington, J. (1993) 'Your nature of science profile: An activity for science teachers, *School Science Review.* **Pages 270, 109–112.**

RELATIVISM/POSITIVISM

Relativist

You deny that things are true or false solely based on an independent reality. The 'truth' of a theory will depend on the norms and rationality of the social group considering it as well as the experimental techniques used to test it. Judgements as to the truth of scientific theories will vary from individual to individual and from one culture to another i.e. truth is relative not absolute.

Positivist

You believe strongly that scientific knowledge is more 'valid' than other forms of knowledge. The laws and theories generated by experiments are our descriptions of patterns we see in a real, external objective world.

To the positivist, science is the primary source of truth. Positivism recognises empirical facts and observable phenomena as the raw material of science. The scientist's job is to establish the objective relationships between the laws governing the facts and observables. Positivism rejects inquiry into underlying causes and ultimate origins.

INDUCTIVISM/DEDUCTIVISM

Inductivism

You believe that the scientist's job is the interrogation of nature. By observing many particular instances, one is able to infer from the particular to the general and then determine the underlying laws and theories.

According to inductivism, scientists generalise from a set of observations to a universal law 'inductively'. Scientific knowledge is built by induction from a secure set of observations.

Deductivism

In our definition this means that you believe that scientists proceed by testing ideas produced by the logical consequences of current theories or of their bold imaginative ideas.

According to deductivism (or hypothetico-deductivism) scientific reasoning consists of the forming of hypotheses which are not established by the empirical data but may be suggested by them. Science then proceeds by testing the observable consequences of these hypotheses, i.e. observations are directed or led by hypotheses – they are theory laden.

CONTEXTUALISM/DECONTEXTUALISM

Contextualism

You hold the view that the truth of scientific knowledge and processes is interdependent with the culture in which the scientists live and in which it takes place.

Decontextualism

You hold the view that scientific knowledge is independent of its cultural location and sociological structure.

PROCESS/CONTENT

Process

You see science as a characteristic set of identifiable methods/processes. The learning of these is the essential part of science education.

Content

You think that science is characterised by the facts and ideas it has and that the essential part of science education is the acquisition and mastery of this 'body of knowledge'.

INSTRUMENTALISM/REALISM

Instrumentalism

You believe that scientific theories and ideas are fine if they work, that is they allow correct predictions to be made. They are instruments which we can use but they say nothing about an independent reality on their own truth.

Realism

You believe that scientific theories are statements about a world that exists in space and time independent of the scientists' perceptions. Correct theories describe things which are really there, independent of the scientists, e.g. atoms.

Analysis

As we saw earlier, the nature of science is an important part of any science curriculum. However, as a teacher, your view of the nature of science is likely to differ from that of both your colleagues and pupils. It is important that all teachers and learners are aware of possible differences and that, unlike most of the science curriculum, there is neither a universal view of the nature of science nor a 'correct answer'.

The following activity is aimed at a critical consideration of your views of the nature of science but should not be seen as an objective measure.

Personal response

Having read the contrasting views listed above, decide which of them you agree with.

Practical implications and activities

- Answer the questions below and record your results.
- Discuss with your peers how your assessment compares with both their own assessment and with your self assessment.

Your Nature of Science Profile

(Adapted from Nott, M. and Wellington, J. (1993) 'Your nature of science profile: An activity for science teachers', *SSR*, 75 (270), 109–112)

Please read each of these statements carefully. Give each one a number ranging from 'Strongly agree' (+5) to 'Strongly disagree' (–5) and place it next to the statement. A score of 0 will indicate a balanced view. For the moment, ignore the initials in brackets.

1. The results that pupils get from their experiments are as valid as anybody else's. (RP)
2. Science is essentially a masculine construct. (CD)
3. Science facts are what scientists agree that they are. (CD, RP)
4. The object of scientific activity is to reveal reality. (IR)
5. Scientists have no idea of the outcome of an experiment before they do it. (ID)
6. Scientific research is economically and politically determined. (CD)
7. Science education should be more about the learning of scientific processes than the learning of scientific facts. (PC)
8. The processes of science are divorced from moral and ethical considerations. (CD)
9. The most valuable part of a scientific education is what remains after the facts have been forgotten. (PC)
10. Scientific theories are valid if they work. (IR)
11. Science proceeds by drawing generalisable conclusions (which later become theories) from available data. (ID)
12. There is such a thing as a true scientific theory. (RP, IR)
13. Human emotion plays no part in the creation of scientific knowledge. (CD)
14. Scientific theories describe a real external world which is independent of human perception. (RP, IR)
15. A good solid grounding in basic scientific facts and inherited scientific knowledge is essential before young scientists can go on to make discoveries of their own. (PC)
16. Scientific theories have changed over time simply because experimental techniques have improved. (RP, CD)
17. 'Scientific method' is transferable from one scientific investigation to another. (PC)
18. In practice, choices between competing theories are made purely on the basis of experimental results. (CD, RP)
19. Scientific theories are as much a result of imagination and intuition as inference from experimental results. (ID)
20. Scientific knowledge is different from other kinds of knowledge in that it has higher status. (RP)
21. There are certain physical events in the universe which science can never explain. (RP, IR)
22. Scientific knowledge is morally neutral – only the application of knowledge is ethically determined. (CD)
23. All scientific experiments and observations are determined by existing theories. (ID)
24. Science is essentially characterised by the methods and processes it uses (PC)

Nature of Science Profile scoring instructions

Put your score for each question in the appropriate box(es) below.

Some questions score twice.

Some 'scores' have to have their sign REVERSED before they can be used; this is indicated by a '–' next to the number, e.g. if your response to statement 1 is –3, then the score in the right-hand column on the RP box will be +3.

RP		
Statement		Score
1	(–)	
3	(–)	
21	(–)	
12	(+)	
14	(+)	
16	(+)	
18	(+)	
20	(+)	
Total		

ID		
Statement		Score
5	(–)	
11	(–)	
19	(+)	
23	(+)	
Total		

CD		
Statement		Score
2	(–)	
3	(–)	
6	(–)	
8	(–)	
13	(+)	
16	(+)	
18	(+)	
22	(+)	
Total		

PC		
Statement		Score
7	(–)	
9	(–)	
17	(–)	
24	(–)	
15	(+)	
Total		

IR		
Statement		Score
10	(–)	
21	(+)	
4	(+)	
12	(+)	
14	(+)	
Total		

Add up the scores in the right-hand columns to give you a grand total for each grid.

N.B. Some statements score positive, some negative.

Transfer the marks from the columns to the position on each relevant axis. Join up the 5 marks. This is your profile at this moment.

Relativism   **Positivism**

–40 –36 –32 –28 –24 –20 –16 –12 –8 –4 **RP** 4 8 12 16 20 24 28 32 36 40

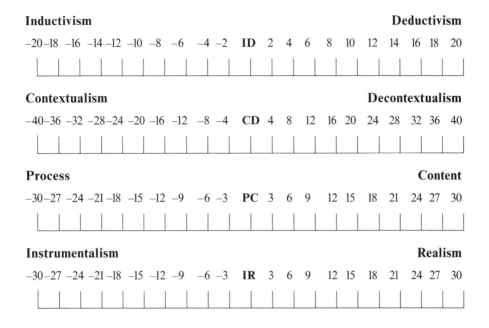

Inductivism | Deductivism

−20 −18 −16 −14 −12 −10 −8 −6 −4 −2 **ID** 2 4 6 8 10 12 14 16 18 20

Contextualism | Decontextualism

−40 −36 −32 −28 −24 −20 −16 −12 −8 −4 **CD** 4 8 12 16 20 24 28 32 36 40

Process | Content

−30 −27 −24 −21 −18 −15 −12 −9 −6 −3 **PC** 3 6 9 12 15 18 21 24 27 30

Instrumentalism | Realism

−30 −27 −24 −21 −18 −15 −12 −9 −6 −3 **IR** 3 6 9 12 15 18 21 24 27 30

How

Before you read this extract, read:

- Monk, M. and Dillon, J. (2000) 'The Nature of Scientific Knowledge', in Monk, M. and Osborne, J. (eds) *Good Practice in Science Teaching.* Buckingham: Open University Press (pp. 78–81).

Extract: Sorsby, B. (2000) in Sears, J. and Sorensen, P. (eds) *Issues in Science Education.* London: Routledge. Pages 26–27.

The finding that NoS is generally not taught in the classroom is serious, but there is currently a lack of emphasis on NoS as a subject in the training of science teachers too (see for example: Palmquist and Finley 1997). In addition there are only a few examples in the research literature about how the situation might be remedied for pre-service and in-service teachers, although there are occasional descriptions of undergraduate education courses (for example in the review by Matthews 1994).

How can we approach teaching NoS to both adults and children? Lipman (1988: 27) considered that 'by and large teachers should be taught by the very same procedures as those they are expected to employ in the classroom'. Lipman's view underpins the following section, and approaches to teaching NoS to both pupils and teachers are considered in tandem.

Teaching and learning about the nature of science can be approached through philosophical contexts, especially using methodologies which involve argumentation. Working from a teacher education perspective, Lipman (1988) presented a three-stage strategy for developing a greater awareness of pedagogical approaches to philosophical issues namely, curriculum exploration, modelling and observation/ classroom research. It is clear that at all stages discussion, logical argument and persuasion are vital. For child and adult learners alike, it is important to give time and structures to explore the nature of science through dialogue, and discussion both in science and about science (Sorsby 1996b, 1999c, Newton et al., 1999)

A second approach draws on sociological studies of the nature of science and this involves bringing out the relevance of science to pupils and to teachers. For some aspects such as ecology and health related issues, it is relatively straightforward to place the science within a human context. In other areas, such as those typically associated with the physical sciences, the human connections are less obvious, but in all, the role of discussion and argumentation is again very important. Ratcliffe (1998) recommended the following approaches to ensure good practice in science lessons: clarify the purpose of the discussion; make the science base overt; emphasise the nature of the evidence; use a framework for analysing discussion; value pupils' opinions; group pupils carefully; review the activity.

The longest-established approach uses socio-historical case studies to help pupils understand the nature of science and these may cover both biographical and thematic studies and some good support materials for schools have been produced (see for example Shortland and Warwick 1989, Solomon 1991, Honey 1990 and Nott 1994). There is also available a thrice-yearly pack of photocopiable teacher resources. 'Breakthrough', which was reviewed very favourably by Buss (1999).

Historical and science-in-society approaches for pupils have much in common. They share a pedagogy with Lipman's approach to teaching philosophy which includes discussion about socio-historical case studies; reading about science and science in society issues (especially from primary resources); listening to and watching audio visual presentations; using dramatic reconstructions of social and historical conflicts where science is involved; replicating historical experiments; simulation and role-play. Experience shows that it is reasonably straightforward to transfer some of these approaches, especially reading and discussion, to programmes for pre-service and in-service education of teachers and other adults. There are, however, greater challenges with getting adult learners to become involved in role-play and drama, especially on in-service courses where participants are unlikely to know each other sufficiently well for the approach to be successful. A successful approach using a limited degree of role-play with adult learners uses argumentation around history of science case studies. The teachers as a whole group are reminded (or taught) the basics of a current scientific theory, and as a group they have to identify and marshal evidence to support that theory.

The tutor adopts the stance of propounding an alternative theory, and uses the data gathered by the teachers, as well as additional data, to provide an evidence base for the alternative theory. For example, in a historical case study of the oxygen versus phlogiston theories of burning, teachers are asked to provide data from a series of practical exercises to establish what is observed and measured when burning takes place. The tutor provides a counter-blast to the teachers' evidence and provides additional evidence, which can be used to support the phlogiston theory. Other case studies have involved the heliocentric versus the geocentric theories and the four-element theory of matter versus the atomic theory. In all of these, the aim is to illuminate for the teachers more about the nature of science, and especially to emphasise the role of argumentation in the processes of science.

Another approach to NoS, is through open ended investigations in science which involve problem solving. Practical investigations in science are well established in both primary and secondary pupils' education, and experience has shown that this is a successful approach with teacher education too.

Analysis

It can be seen from the extract that learning and teaching about the nature of science may draw on philosophical, sociological and historical approaches. Often these approaches are unfamiliar to the trainee science teacher and, as such, we would argue that it is imperative for trainees to be given the opportunity to model classroom delivery to their peers prior to actual delivery in the classroom.

As with any topic, the range of modes of delivery is only limited by the teacher's creativity (resources permitting). The following activity, it is hoped, will allow you and your peers to explore this creativity.

Personal response

Look back on your own learning and teaching experience and reflect on opportunities for, and examples of, learning and teaching about the nature of science.

Practical implications and activities

For each of the categories identified in the extract above (philosophical, sociological, historical) plan, with a colleague, how you could address those elements of the nature of science as an integral part of a Key Stage 3 or Key Stage 4 topic.

Further reading

Barrow, J. (1998) *The World Within the World*. Oxford: Oxford University Press.

Chalmers, A. (1976) *What is this Thing Called Science?* Buckingham: Open University Press.

Harrison, A.G. (2002) 'John Dalton's Atomic Theory: Using the history and nature of science to teach particle concepts'. Paper presented at the Annual Meeting of Australian Association for Research in Education. Brisbane, Australia. Available on-line at: http://www.aare.edu.au/02pap/har02049.htm

Okasha, S. (2002) *The Philosophy of Science: A Very Short Introduction*. Oxford: Oxford University Press.

9 Citizenship and ethical issues in science education

By the end of this chapter you should have considered and reflected upon:

- **what** is understood by citizenship in science education;
- **why** citizenship and ethical issues should be considered when planning for learning and teaching in science;
- **how** learning and teaching episodes, in science, can be developed which address inclusion and special needs.

Linking your learning
Achieving QTS Reflective Reader: Secondary Professional Studies. Hoult, S. (2005), pages 140–143.

Professional Standards for QTS
1.1, 1.8, 2.2, 2.4, 3.3.2c, 3.3.2d

Introduction

A number of issues arising from the delivery of science will contribute to the wider development of pupils in the school. Just as literacy and numeracy are whole-school issues to which science can make a major contribution. The same view can be taken of ethical issues and citizenship also addressed through science. Issues of common debate, which draw on science, in the media, for example BSE, HIV, GM foods and more recently avian influenza, impact on all members of society or citizens. Other issues which are rooted in science, for example animal experimentation, organ transplantation and nuclear weapons programmes, raise ethical objections amongst a sizable minority (and in some cases a majority). With this in mind some may argue that 'socio-scientific' issues is perhaps a better term than both citizenship and ethical issues, and whilst this term may be even more wide ranging than what is to be discussed here, they both share a common view of being based in science and potentially impacting on society.

Citizenship is a statutory part of the National Curriculum for England and Wales, from 2002 at Key Stage 3 and 2004 at Key Stage 4. However, unlike other statutory components of the National Curriculum, the eight-level scale is not in place but end-of-stage descriptors are available at Key Stages 3 and 4. In addition, for those schools and pupils who deem it appropriate, a short-course GCSE is available which recognises pupil achievement.

In addition, all trainee teachers need to demonstrate competence in the standards, which include the National Curriculum framework and 14–19 pathways and assessments.

It is our contention, however, that best practice in science teaching will include planning for such issues and allowing pupils to arrive at an informed decision in a supportive and unthreatening environment without the need for external pressures to drive them.

In this chapter you with reflect on a definition of citizenship, why it is an important part of best practice and how you can develop effective approaches for its delivery.

What

What is citizenship? This is a difficult concept to pin down, as Ratcliffe and Grace (2003) suggest, 'citizenship is a contested and slippery concept'. Heater (1999) suggests:

> Citizens need knowledge and understanding of the social, legal and political system(s) in which they operate. They need skills and aptitudes to make use of that knowledge and understanding. And they need to be endowed with values and dispositions to put their knowledge and skills to beneficial use.

Citizenship in schools or citizenship education is a fairly recent phenomenon, with the QCA (1998) stating that:

> Citizenship education must be education for citizenship. It is not an end in itself, even if it will involve learning a body of knowledge, as well as the development of skills and values.

The approach to citizenship education which became part of the statutory orders for the National Curriculum began with the Crick Report (QCA, 1998). The Crick Report identified three elements which should inform citizenship education:

- community involvement;
- political literacy;
- social and moral responsibility.

Whilst it may not be immediately obvious that these three elements map onto the secondary school science curriculum, further analysis may make matters clearer.

Community involvement is being part of the school, tutor group or science class. Professional scientists (and science teachers) are part of their academic and professional communities. Research scientists are evermore involved in large-scale projects with multinational teams; these are part of a community. However we define 'community', pupils need to be aware that membership of the community brings with it responsibilities and duties to the community (see Blandford, 2000).

Political literacy need not be simply the understanding of the political system, be it democratic or not, since this could be seen as too narrow. Political literacy is perhaps better taken to be the development of those *political skills* of debate, decision-making and critical and strategic thinking. Scientific research operates in this way, as indeed do policy and curriculum developments in science education. Pupils in school can be engaged with scientific concepts via the use of mock debate, thus developing their personal *political literacy*.

Social and moral responsibility can also be addressed via science education. Typical examples could be environmental education, renewable energy and animal testing. The way in which we interact with each other, especially regarding these issues, is governed by our *values*. Did the development of the first atomic bomb ultimately save lives by bringing the Second World War to a swift end or cost lives by being detonated? Much depends on our values, or social responsibility, as does much of science. Indeed, Robert Oppenheimer, who led the development of the atomic bomb, is often quoted as saying: 'Scientists cannot hold back progress for fear of what man may do with it'. This is a big question but one which, we argue, is open to secondary school science pupils.

Ethical issues, considering the above, cannot be divorced from citizenship education. One could argue that moral decisions, and indeed social responsibility, are driven by our ethics. It could be further argued that both ethics and science share a similar definition. For example Fullick and Ratcliffe (1996) offer:

> *Science: the process of rational enquiry which seeks to propose explanations for observations of natural phenomena.*
> *Ethics: the process of rational enquiry by which we decide on issues right (good) and wrong (bad) as applied to people and their actions.*

Since science is a human construct, all science must apply to people and their actions, hence science must involve the application of ethical processes. Ethics often sparks the idea of a controversial issue. Wellington (1986) argues that a controversial issue must involve value judgements which cannot be settled by facts, evidence or experimentation alone and it must be considered important by an appreciable number of people. This is echoed by the Crick Report (QCA, 1998), where controversial issues are defined as ones for which there is no universally held point of view, which commonly divide society and for which significant groups offer conflicting explanations and solutions. Is this not the way science evolves, for example the change from a heliocentric universe, the plum-pudding model of the atom or the corpuscular theory of light?

Personal response

How would you define:
a. citizenship
b. education for citizenship
c. ethical issues?

Practical implications and activities

- During your school-based placement arrange to meet with the co-ordinator for citizenship. Discuss with the co-ordinator the whole-school policy on citizenship and compare it with your definitions.
- With your school-based mentor discuss how citizenship is integrated into the scheme of work for science. How does this match the whole school policy?

Why

In the previous section we raised two points: it is a National Curriculum requirement and trainee teachers need to show competence in order to achieve Qualified Teacher Status (QTS).

Whilst these two points may be taken as given, we hope to have newly qualified teachers who are reflective practitioners. So, we would look for something more than being able to 'tick the box'. If we have science as a statutory requirement from age 5 to 16 then it must prepare pupils, including those who do not study science post-16, for life. Life is evermore dependent on science or its application and in order to play a full part in society members of that society need to be able to engaged with the issues affecting it. Lord Dearing expresses this as:

> *Democracy is more fragile than people realise. The quality of democracy depends on engagement by the people. If you look for ways of encouraging participation, it is scientific contexts that you will find the issues which will really grab young people.*
>
> (Lord Dearing, 2002. http://www.wellcome.ac.uk/node5930.html)

Before you read the following extract, read:

- Kitson, A. (2004) 'Citizenship', in Brooks, V., Abbott, I. and Bill, L. (eds) *Preparing to Teach in Secondary Schools*. Buckingham: Open University Press.

Extract: Ratcliffe, M. and Grace, M. (2003) *Science education for citizenship*. Open University Press. Pages 1–3.

Many areas of debate in the media and in social policy relate to socio-scientific issues. As we write this the news headlines are on the radio – they include the Irish government campaigning against a new nuclear reprocessing plant because of radioactive pollution; concerns about the way in which the British foot-and-mouth outbreak had been handled; DNA evidence in a murder trial. These are typical socio-scientific issues which reach national prominence. They can impact on individuals and groups at different levels, from determining policy through to individual decision-making.

Most people are interested in *applications* of science and technology. In 1999, the Office of Science and Technology (OST) and the Wellcome Trust collaborated in research designed to explore attitudes towards science, technology and engineering. As part of the study they surveyed a stratified random location sample of 1839 representative British adults for their interest in particular topics (OST/Wellcome 2000). Almost all were interested in health issues and new medical discoveries (91 per cent and 87 per cent respectively). More people were interested in environmental issues (82 per cent), new inventions and technologies (74 per cent) and new scientific discoveries (71 per cent) than in sport (60 per cent), politics (55 per cent) and economics (48 per cent). Although there are no comparable data for children and adolescents, a declared public interest in science has been shown in previous opinion-poll data of this type (Durant et al., 1989).

It is perhaps safe to assume that scientific issues will continue to interest future generations. However, it is notable that in the focus group discussions, as a complementary part of this large-scale research, little interest was expressed in the abstract concepts of science – those largely present in the school science curriculum (OST/Wellcome 2000). Participants were more inclined to discuss the benefits, applications and social use of science and technology. The survey showed that 'interest in a specific area of science is highly correlated with the perceived benefit'. In rating some (given) scientific topics, medical advances and telecommunications which were seen of great benefit were viewed with the most interest. The relationship between science as perceived in the school curriculum – the mastery of some fundamental science concepts – and that of interest and use in adulthood is not a straightforward one. Layton and others (1993) showed that adults use situated scientific knowledge for specific purposes – in which an important aspect is the way scientific concepts are explored in a context specific to the issue under consideration. For example, in dealing with the problems of caring for their Down's syndrome children, parents used their practical knowledge integrated with scientific knowledge they gained from this experience rather than authoritative scientific information given to them formally by experts. Interest and motivation seem high when socio-scientific issues are addressed.

The nature of socio-scientific issues

The authors go on to show that socio-scientific issues:

- have a basis in science, frequently that at the frontiers of scientific knowledge;
- involve forming opinions, making choices at personal or societal level;
- are frequently media-reported, with attendant issues of presentation based on the purposes of the communicator;
- deal with incomplete information because of conflicting/incomplete scientific evidence, and inevitably incomplete reporting;
- address local, national and global dimensions with attendant political and societal frameworks;
- involve some cost-benefit analysis in which risk interacts with values;
- may involve consideration of sustainable development;
- involve values and ethical reasoning;
- may require some understanding of probability and risk;
- are frequently topical with a transient life.

Analysis

In this extract the authors draw on the interest in applications of science rather than specific science content. The fact that adults draw on science knowledge they have 'gained through experience' in specific situations rather than from 'authoritative scientific' sources should suggest to us, as science educators, that providing the skills to enable them to do so effectively is at least as important as 'the mastery of fundamental science concepts'.

In listing the nature of socio-scientific issues, which you will recall from the above is an alternative term for citizenship and/or ethical issues, the extract gives ten reasons for including them in science education. A number of these reasons offer direct support for the National Curriculum and in particular ones which address scientific enquiry:

- deal with incomplete information because of conflicting/incomplete scientific evidence, and inevitably incomplete reporting;
- may require some understanding of probability and risk.

It is often the case, in the quest to complete the content, that this area of National Curriculum science, and hence anything which feeds into this aspect, must be an advantage.

In addition, a number feed into cross-curricular issues, for example:

- may involve sustainable development, which links to design and technology;
- address local, national and global dimensions with attendant political and societal frameworks, which links into the citizenship and PHSE curricula.

These two, as with the others, can be mapped onto many aspects of science as discussed above.

Personal response

Considering all that you have read, here and elsewhere, and your experience in school why do you think socio-scientific issues should be integrated into your science teaching?

Practical implications and activities

Working with your school-based mentor and/or a colleague, take the ten bullet points in the extract and attempt to place them against aspects of the science National Curriculum.
Working with your school-based mentor, consider how many of the ten points are explicitly addressed in the school's scheme of work.

How

Having considered what and why, we need to consider how citizenship and ethical issues can be addressed in science.

At the whole-school level the Crick Report expected that five per cent of curriculum time be given over to citizenship and that it could be delivered in blocks, modules, tutor time, discrete periods, general studies programmes or through existing subjects.

In this section we will consider the 'through existing subjects' approach which, in addition to adding to the whole-school provision, can enhance science learning and teaching. Everington (2004) offers the following contributions that science can make to spiritual, moral and cultural development:

- spiritual development: role of scientific discoveries in changing people's lives and thinking;
- moral development: why sustainable development is important;
- cultural development: relationship between culture and nature of scientific exploration.

This advice does not, however, lead to practical teaching resources. Unfortunately it would appear that when such material is provided it is not always taken up with enthusiasm; in fact the enthusiasm with which teachers take up the available resources is related to the following issues:

- their relevance to science teaching issues 'of the moment';
- their immediate applicability to classroom practice;
- their intrinsic interest.

(Adapted from Ratcliffe and Grace, 2003)

The issue for you, is to generate or assimilate teaching materials, with enthusiasm, into your teaching. To help with this it is worth considering guidance given in *Citizenship: Scheme of Work for KS3 Teacher's Guide* (QCA, 2001), where advantages, disadvantages and implications for delivery through the existing subjects are given. For example:

- advantages: integrated approach gives relevance for learning in the subject;
- disadvantages: co-ordination across departments;
- implications: extra time needed to meet both citizenship and subject objectives.

All three of these go back to what we have written about good practice. We need to give pupils a relevant context to engage them. If we are to have a National Curriculum rather than ten National Curricula we need co-operation and if we are to have anything other than tokenism we need time. The time issue, however, is not all negative since if citizenship is delivered through the subjects then curriculum time is not needed for discrete lessons. This time may then be given over to science, leading to a net gain of time.

In developing a lesson plan which will address citizenship, ethical issues or socio-scientific issues through a science lesson, you should consider the following:

- What is your own view of the nature of science?
- What is your pupils' view of the nature of science?
- What impact does your value system have on your views?
- What impact does your pupils' value systems have on their views?
- How will you share the objectives of the lesson with your pupils?

An example is a Key Stage 3 lesson looking at blood as a transport mechanism.

Name: Luke Walker
Class: 8A
Date: Friday 15th October
Time: Periood 1, 08:50

LESSON PLAN

Administration	NC reference
Register all pupils Have all resources to hand Have pupil groups organised	Sc2 2j, 2l Citizenship KS3 2a, 2b, 3a ICT KS3 3a, 3b, 3c

Pupil learning objectives	Trainee-teacher objectives
• By the end of the lesson pupils will by able to recall the development of blood banking and the use of plasma. • By the end of the lesson pupils will be able to discuss the ethical issues involved including religious objection and the myth regarding blood plasma from different races.	• To be able to organise and deliver a lesson which looks at wider issues in science education.

Time	Teacher/pupil activity	Feedback strategy	Organisation
08:45 08:50	Arrive prior to the class. Meet and greet, coats off, begin starter activity on the whiteboard.		Questions on whiteboard
08:55	Call register whilst pupils work on starter.		
09:00	Go over starter activity.		
09:05	Introduce the development of blood banking during the Second World War and the work of Charles Drew (first black American to receive a DSc).	Self-assessment	
09:15	Split into groups, discuss action of the US Army in asking the Red Cross to separate blood from black and white donors – Drew's resignation.	Intervention questions	Discussion cards
09:25	Use laptops to draft letter of resignation.	Use of science facts	Laptops
09:40	Plenary questions, ethics.		
09:45	Set research homework: the myth around Drew's death and religious objections to transfusions.	Open questions	Homework sheets

Prompts: Equal Opps ✓   Cross-curricular links ✓   Continuity and progression ✓

Homework ✓   Safety na   Differentiation ✓

Personal response

How would you, as a human being and a scientist, have reacted had you been Charles Drew?

Practical implications and activities

With a colleague develop a lesson or series of lessons which would allow you to address an aspect of citizenship or ethical issues in either Key Stage 3 or 4. Having planned the lesson(s) discuss it with your school-based mentor before producing the resources and delivering the lesson.

In your evaluation concentrate on how well the pupil learning objectives have been met.

Further reading

Blandford, S. (2006) *Remodelling of Schools*. London: Pearson.

DfES/QCA (1999) *Citizenship*. Norwich: HMSO.

Osler, A. and Strakey, M. (2005) *Changing Citizenship*. Buckingham: Open University Press.

Ratcliffe, M. and Grace, M. (2003) *Science Education for Citizenship*. Buckingham: Open University Press.

10 Thinking skills in science

By the end of this chapter you will have considered and reflected upon:

- **what** approaches to teaching thinking skills exist;
- the psychological argument for **why** we should introducing thinking skills lessons into schools;
- an outline of **how** the CASE approach to thinking skills is used in secondary science lessons.

Linking your learning
Achieving QTS. Reflective Reader: Secondary Professional Studies. Hoult, S. (2005) Chapter 2.

Professional Standards for QTS
1.1, 1.2, 2.1c, 2.4, 3.2.4, 3.2.5, 3.3.3

Introduction

Each successive summer, when school examination results are published, if there is an improvement in the proportion of pupils gaining higher grades then one can guarantee that some politician or other will be putting forward the argument that this was as a result of the examinations getting easier. Conversely, if there is a marginal reduction in the proportion of higher grades, this will be accompanied by claims of falling standards in schools. The temptation is to consider such assertions to be unsubstantiated political rhetoric. However, the findings of a shortly-to-be-published, large-scale study, carried out by Michael Shayer, involving 10,000 Year 7 pupils (*Education Guardian*, 24 January 2006) would appear to give some substance to these assertions. Reported in the article are the claims that Year 7 pupils are now on average between two and three years behind what they were 15 years ago in terms of cognitive development. Admittedly, one has to make a value judgement as to whether the tests used in the most recent study or those used in public examinations are more worthwhile: do they measure what is important or what does not matter? However, if the recent results are to be believed, a worrying situation exists.

Why

Contrary to the findings of Shayer, official government figures would appear to support the argument that children in primary schools are improving and, in a press release (DfES, August 2004) supporting this belief, the School Standards Minister, David Miliband, said that:

primary schools are getting better again following this year's test results for 11-year-olds. And he said the evidence shows that schools in some of the poorest areas in England are catching up the rest.

Further supporting this claim, the official DfES site goes on to state that:

At age 11, Key Stage 2, a record 77% of pupils achieved the expected level in English, an increase of 2 percentage points from last year (up 12 percentage points compared to 1998), and 74% of pupils achieved the expected level in maths, a 1 percentage point increase from last year (up 15 percentage points from 6 years ago).

Can the statistics cited above and the findings of Shayer both be correct?

Personal response

- Consider the statements referred to above and those in the introduction. Can both views be correct? Can you suggest an explanation for this dichotomy?

Practical implications and activities

Consult the Local Education Authority website for either your current or previous placement school and extract the published data for Key Stage 2 or Key Stage 3 Science National Curriculum test results for the school's main feeder primary school(s). Do these data support either Shayer or Milliband's views concerning achievement?

If we only partly accept the argument of Shayer, the development of children in England gives considerable cause for concern. Is there anything that can be done to improve the situation?

Consider the following problem:

Jane is taller than Helen.
Helen is taller than Susan.
Who is the tallest?

To the reader, this is a seemingly simple problem. However, to a pre-school child, a solution may be impossible.

In order to solve such a problem, somehow the two relationships have to be combined. Drawing upon the work of Case (1991), an argument could be made that young children encode and interpret information so slowly that the first idea has begun to decay before the second can be absorbed. An alternative argument, based upon processing capacity (Halford, 1992), would be that the young children do not yet have the mental capacity to retain two ideas simultaneously in their minds. In both cases, the result is that the child is unable to combine the two ideas and solve the problem.

Whether the reader favours one theory over the other, it is apparent that an ability to master certain concepts comes with maturity and it is possible to construct a hierarchy of concept development (Shayer and Adey, 1981; Twidle, 2006). One interpretation of this developmental position is somewhat deterministic: 'Lucy has not yet developed sufficiently to be able to handle the idea, so don't waste your time trying to teach her it.' This approach would take the form of a rather crude matching idea that individuals should only be presented with material that matched their current stage of development. However, Adey and Shayer (1994, p. 7) would argue that:

> *A deliberate policy of challenging learners to transcend their present level of thinking not only accelerates their rate of intellectual development, but also in the long term brings about the achievements which a matching policy on its own would have denied them.*

How then can this be done? What sort of approach can achieve this goal?

What

'Thinking skills' is an umbrella term for a range of intellectual powers that would include critical thinking, logic, philosophical enquiry and problem-solving. Many would argue that such skills can be fostered through a range of carefully designed activities and that any improvement would help pupils achieve their full potential as thinkers, with the result that their performance in a range of intellectual activities should improve. Science lessons, taught appropriately, may be the ideal vehicle to foster such development and the authors of the National Curriculum for science (DfEE, 1999, p. 9) acknowledged this when they wrote that 'science provides opportunities to promote thinking skills, through pupils engaging in the process of scientific enquiry'.

Within schools, there are three different approaches to the teaching of such skills, namely:

- programmes that target general thinking skills and are usually timetabled separately;
- programmes that are subject- (for example, science or maths) or domain-specific;
- an approach that incorporates thinking skills across the curriculum.

Personal response

Consider the approaches to thinking skills activities listed above and try to think of advantages and disadvantages to each approach. Discuss your ideas with those of a colleague.

Practical implications and activities

- Inspect the National Curriculum document for science and identify the areas that you believe could be used to develop pupils' thinking skills.
- Consider the programmes outlined below and try to decide which of the above three approaches would be best suited for their delivery.

In addition to the approaches noted above, the Department for Education and Skills (DfES) further categorises the programmes as cognitive intervention, brain-based approaches and philosophical approaches.

Cognitive intervention

Psychological theories, such as those of Jean Piaget (1972) and Lev Vygotsky (1978), have been influential in the development of a number of such programmes and a feature common to such approaches is that specific activities, which can be taught, have been developed with the aim of improving general cognitive functions. Cognitive Acceleration through Science Education (CASE), the brainchild of Philip Adey, Michael Shayer and Carolyn Yates (1995), is a well-evaluated, successful and popular programme that focuses upon the development of scientific thinking in Year 7 and 8 pupils. Positive results have been reported of enhanced pupils' success in public examinations not only in science subjects but also in maths and English (see below for a more detailed consideration of this approach).

Another psychologically based approach, the earlier 'Instrumental Enrichment' (IE) of Reuven Feuerstein (1980), was designed, over a period of two or more years, to enhance the intellectual processing skills, motivation and self-concept of disadvantaged Middle Eastern teenage immigrants to Israel. Instrumental enrichment programmes have since been used with a wider age range and have shown positive effects on non-verbal reasoning (McGuinness, 1999).

The 'Somerset Thinking Skills' course (Blagg et al. 1988), an English development of IE, is another intervention programme which has been used with success (McGuinness, 1999) with a broader ability range and has been extended into occupational settings.

Brain-based approaches

Research into how the human brain works has been drawn upon to develop such approaches. For example, Edward De Bono has argued in favour of using an understanding of brain mechanisms in order to construct approaches to teaching. De Bono's (1976) Cognitive Research Trust (CoRT) programme consists of 60 lessons intended to be used with children from the age of 12 years, although it has been used in adult management training where the approach of focusing upon strategies to foster divergent thinking make it intuitively attractive. Edwards (1991) has reviewed a number of evaluations of CoRT but has, however, been critical of their design, and this led Adey and Shayer (1994), whilst praising the programme for its consideration of important aspects of thinking, to give a verdict on its effectiveness as 'unproven'. A more recent study of the benefits of CoRT (Ritchie and Edwards, 1996) reports that, whilst creative thinking can be taught through this approach, success in CoRT lessons is not enough to produce more generalised gains and that they did not significantly affect cognitive ability.

Philosophical approaches

The emphasis in these approaches is on questioning and reasoning, where a question or issue is identified which might be solved or explained through discussion by a group. The teacher supports or challenges the reasoning and discussion. Matthew Lipman's 'Philosophy for Children' (1980) has been used in the context of moral and social education and evaluations (McGuinness, 1999) have shown positive effects in standard achievement tests as well as enhancing children's discussion and argumentative skills.

Extract: Adey, P. and Shayer, M. (2002) Cognitive acceleration comes of age in Adey, P. and Shayer, M. *Learning intelligence*. Pages 1–3.

Cognitive Acceleration (CA) has come of age in the sense of growing out from its roots in secondary school science into all areas of the curriculum and across the school age range. We may claim immodestly that this proliferation has come about through the efforts of the authors represented in this volume and others, but must recognise also that the current political and social climate is generally friendly to the growth of programmes which develop higher level thinking abilities. It has become a truism that modern society has very little place for unthinking manual labour and that every school leaver needs to be equipped with flexible thinking skills developed to their maximum capacity, and this is now a tenet of the British Government's educational policy. Although Nisbet's (1993) prediction that 'before the century is out, no curriculum will be regarded as acceptable unless it can be shown to make a contribution to the teaching of thinking' has not quite been fulfilled, it is the case that the National Curriculum (NC) for England now does include the development of thinking as a central requirement. We may quibble about the particularities of the 'thinking skills' specified, but it would be churlish not to recognise the real political will that schools should be required to attend directly to students' intellectual development, beyond the requirements of mastering particular bodies of information. We are convinced that some 80 per cent of the school population currently perform academically well below their potential, yet by means of suitable intervention virtually all can function at levels where presently only the top 20 per cent lie.

In this book we will show how such interventions are being worked out in a wide variety of curricula and age contexts. Our original context-delivered interventions were aimed at the 12- to 14-year-old group and were focused on the two most cognitively demanding of the school subjects: science and mathematics. In discussion of their pedagogies, understandably the emphasis was on promoting thinking. Yet one has only to hear an already skilled child musician, or see the drawings of a child with an artistic gift, to realise that the ability to exhibit a high degree of integrated processing of reality is in no way confined to the context of mathematics or science. Without buying Gardner's (1993) model of Multiple Intelligences, it is easily possible to view in these sophisticated performances 'intelligence-in-action', just as much as in the performance of a child with good mathematical ability. Chapter 9 will describe the Wigan Arts, Reasoning and Thinking Skills (ARTS) project, where the emphasis is on promoting those aspects of superior performance that Arts specialists habitually use to judge and differentiate the performances of their pupils. The recent Cognitive Acceleration in Technology Education (CATE) project, promotes intelligence-in-action in the context of design and technology.

Evidence suggests that the differential between children's potential and their performance is already present at the age of 5, so one of the interventions to be described (CASE@KS1) addresses 5- to 6-year-olds. At this age, school subjects are not so differentiated as they are by the end of primary school, so the CASE@KS1 intervention is rooted in general mental abilities and not set in a particular subject context.

Later we will describe the working out of CA principles in mathematics in Years 5 and 6, where the requirements of the particular subject need to be delivered within a primary school setting, that is by a class teacher rather than a specialist mathematician.

Subsequently we will take a slightly different perspective, showing how some of the skills involved in intervention teaching can be applied usefully to regular science lessons with a benefit to pupils' comprehension, and possibly also to their motivation. Although this seems like blurring the model, it can also be looked on as giving teachers more conscious control of their professional skills in general. Finally, we will offer a theoretical integration of the Piagetian and Vygotskyan foundation on which the whole CA enterprise is founded.

We will revisit the psychological roots of CA and the 'six pillars' of CA which arise from its underlying theory, and recapitulate some of the evidence for the effect of the methods on students. This is partly for the benefit of readers new to CA, but we hope that old CA groupies will benefit from seeing the most recent expression of these fundamental principles. We will finish by raising the possibility that CA actually offers a new paradigm for education.

Theory base
Here are three basic hypotheses on which all CA interventions are based:

1 it is valid to work on the basis of some *general* intellectual function in children which underlies any particular context (subject)-dependent component;
2 this general intellectual function develops with age; and
3 the development of this general intellectual function is influenced both by the environment and by maturation.

Analysis

As detailed in this extract, the principles of CASE teaching have been adopted and adapted by diverse subjects and age ranges. Is it then that the 'S' of CASE is not an essential component? That the approach has been successfully integrated into mathematics teaching is perhaps not surprising. However, if cognitive acceleration had remained within the realms of maths and science, there may have been a risk of this region of the curriculum taking on the role once occupied by a study of the classics.

Adey (1997) rejects the idea that science should become the recommended agent for developing general thinking ability and argues that, although science was the first context through which cognitive acceleration was delivered, there is no reason to believe that any major school subject could not be a vehicle for the development of thinking skills. Shayer (1999), not surprisingly, in support of this stance, argues that it is not the subject matter but the 'CASE method' which unlocks the potential within our children. Some may be tempted to 'lift' activities from the 'Thinking Science' material in order to enhance existing schemes of work. That this approach may result in more interesting and challenging lessons is a strong possibility. However, Shayer (1999) argues that it is not the individual components that make CASE a success but the 'Thinking Science' method espoused by teachers as a result of their extended training.

How

In the UK, it is likely that the CASE programme is the most common example of a thinking skills approach used in secondary schools and it is not uncommon to find elements of the CASE teaching in a significant number of science departments, even those that have not undergone the formal training or adopted the approach in its entirety. As an illustration, at a conservative estimate, around 4,500 science teachers are likely to have had some exposure to training in the CASE approach since its inception in 1991 (Private communication, Adey, 16 April 2004). Although space prevents a detailed consideration of the CASE approach, what follows is an outline of what it entails.

CASE is an approach to science teaching designed by Philip Adey, Michael Shayer and Carolyn Yates (1995) with the intention of raising children's intellectual performance. The CASE 'Thinking Science' curriculum encourages pupils to reflect on their own thinking and to develop their reasoning power in tackling novel problems. The theoretical basis behind CASE builds upon the ideas of development of thinking proposed by Piaget and Vygotsky. The argument given is that pupils, equipped with increased reasoning power, are able to apply this increased reasoning ability to a range of subjects and, hence, score higher in examinations in any academic subject. CASE involves a series of 'Thinking Science' lessons which are designed to be delivered, at regular intervals, over a two year period to pupils in Years 7 and 8.

A typical CASE lesson has five components (the five pillars of CASE), namely:

1. Give the pupils a *concrete experience* that has a regular/predictable pattern; this involves the teacher setting the scene, introducing new equipment and vocabulary.
2. Arrange for an unexpected result that does not agree with the previous pattern or preconceptions (*cognitive conflict*).
3. Encourage the pupils to think and talk about their thinking, consider and share their old/new ideas with each other (*metacognition*).
4. Students construct their *new reasoning process*.
5. Reasoning patterns developed in CASE are *bridged* to other contexts.

At the end of a two-year trial period, students who had experienced the 'Thinking Science' activities showed greater gains in cognitive development than matched control groups. When, in due course, at the age of 16, the trial group completed their GCSE examinations in Year 11, they performed significantly better than the control group, not only in science but also in mathematics and English (Adey and Shayer, 1994; Shayer, 2000). When further teachers had been trained in the process and the exercise was repeated, results showed that schools who adopted CASE methods obtained between 14 and 25 per cent higher grades in science, mathematics and English than non-CASE schools (Shayer, 1996).

Personal response

Think back to your own learning in either school, university or college. Did you ever experience a learning episode in which a CASE-type approach was taken? If so, how did you feel at the time of cognitive conflict?

Practical implications and activities

- Take any topic of your choice from the Key Stage 3 section of the National Curriculum and plan a lesson that includes the five components of a CASE lesson noted above and on your plan, clearly identify where/how the five components are addressed.
- With the approval of the regular class teacher, teach the lesson.
- After the lesson, discuss with the class teacher and/or your mentor issues that arose, paying particular attention to advantages and difficulties that you experienced.

Further reading

Adey, P. and Shayer, M. (1994) *Really Raising Standards*. London: Routledge.

Baumfield, V., Edwards, G., Butterworth, M. and Thacker, D. (2005) *The Impact of the Implementation of Thinking Skills Programmes and Approaches on Teachers*. EPPI-Centre: University of London.

Lee, V. and Das Gupta, P. (1995) *Children's Cognitive and Language Development*. Buckingham: Open University Press.

McGuinness, C. (1999) *From Thinking Skills to Thinking Classrooms*. Nottingham: DfEE Publications.

Shayer, M. and Adey, P. (2002) *Learning Intelligence*. Buckingham: Open University Press.

Wood, D. (1998) *How Children Think and Learn*. Oxford: Blackwell.

11 Classroom research

By the end of this chapter you should have considered and reflected upon:

- **what** is understood by classroom research;
- **why** classroom research is an important tool for developing your teaching and the pupils' learning;
- **how** to go about a small-scale classroom research project.

Linking your learning
Achieving QTS Reflective Reader: Secondary Professional Studies. Hoult, S. (2005) Chapter 11.

Professional Standards for QTS
1.7

Introduction

As with the linking chapter suggested above, from Hoult (2005), this chapter will concentrate on a research paradigm known as 'action-research'. Action research can be described, rather than defined, as:

> *Self-reflective, self-critical and critical enquiry undertaken by professionals to improve the rationality and justice of their own practices.*
>
> (Lomax, 2002)

Action research is also one form of research which can be used in small-scale programmes over short timescales. However, many writers talk of potential problems with action research, especially in terms of validity and reliability of the data collected, with some (e.g. Hopkins, 2002) preferring to talk of classroom research by teachers rather than action research.

In this chapter you will move from a working definition of action research to a discussion of why reflective practice calls on action research, to a sample methodology for carrying it out.

What

As stated in the introduction, action research is undertaken by professionals in order to change the situation under study. This makes it different to other research paradigms where the aim of the research is not to influence the situation.

The following three definitions are presented, not to clarify but to demonstrate the difficulty in capturing such a difficult concept.

> *action research aims to contribute both to the practical concerns of people in an immediate problematic situation and to the goals of social science by joint collaboration.*
>
> (Rapport, 1970)

> *Action research is a form of self reflective enquiry undertaken by participants in social (including educational) situations in order to improve the rationality and justice of (a) their own social or educational practices, (b) their understanding of these practices, and (c) the situations in which practices are carried out.*
>
> (Kemmis, 1983)

> *Action-research might be defined as 'the study of a social situation with a view to improving the quality of action within it'.*
>
> (Elliott, 1991)

Whilst not clarifying a definition of action research, the three definitions, spanning 20 years, all make reference to change of a social situation, in our case an educational one.

So where then do we go with our search for a definition? Just as a physicist would turn to Feynman or a theologian would turn to Peakes, education researchers turn to Cohen and Manion. Now in its fifth edition, with help from Keith Morrison, this work on educational research explains that as a research device action research combines six notions:

1. *a straightforward cycle of: identifying a problem, planning an intervention, implementing the intervention, evaluating the outcome*
2. *reflective practice*
3. *political emancipation*
4. *critical theory*
5. *professional development*
6. *participatory practitioner research.*

(Cohen et al., 2000)

Taking these six notions, we have our working definition of action research as applied to science education.

Personal response

Thinking about research you carried out, or took part in, during your undergraduate or postgraduate study. How does this research compare with the above definitions of action research?

Practical implications and activities

Look back at the six notions given by Cohen et al. and, with a colleague or your mentor, explain your understanding of each notion to each other. Can you come to a consensus? What if you involve your university tutor?

Why

As with most issues in this text we could argue the case for you, the reader, to address this issue as part of your evidence towards Qualified Teacher Status (QTS). However, as we have argued elsewhere, a reflective practitioner should not need external motivation. If we, as educators, are to influence our practice then research is required which draws on our experience as practitioners and define the knowledge base of our subject before outsiders do it for us.

Over 20 years ago Lawrence Stenhouse, without using the term action research, described good teachers as:

> *necessarily autonomous in professional judgement. They do not need to be told what to do. They are not professionally the dependants of researchers or superintendents, innovators or supervisors.*
>
> (Stenhouse, 1984)

Denis Lawton talks, again without using the term, of action research as a way of defining teachers as professionals:

> *The increasing desire of teachers to be treated as professionals rather than as state functionaries, has encouraged a tendency to look for ways in which teachers could solve their own professional problems at a local level rather than react to more remote initiatives.*
>
> (Lawton, 1989)

The following extract looks further into the development of educational research over time from the sixties to the present. Before reading the extract, read:

- Chapter 3 in Hopkins, D. (2002) *A Teacher's Guide to Classroom Research*. Buckingham: Open University Press.

Extract: Gunstone, R. and White, R. (2000) Goals, methods and achievements of research in science education in Millar, R., Leach, J. and Osborne, J. (eds) *Improving Science Education*. Buckingham: Open University Press. Pages 295–297.

Central to research in science education are studies of how effective certain practices are in producing understanding of content. This research has given scholars an increasing appreciation of the complexity of both classrooms and science.

Earlier theories of learning (for example Gagné 1965; Ausubel 1968), and motivation (for example Maslow 1954) treat learners as individuals, with slight attention to their interactions with each other in social groups. A typical study of the 1960s (e.g. Tanner 1969) would attend to the details of teaching procedures being compared, the tests to measure outcomes, and to the statistical analysis of the test scores. It would not attend to the context in which the learning was to occur. It would ignore the feelings of the students for the topic and their prior knowledge of it, their beliefs about the purpose of schooling and about the learning of the topic, and their feelings for each other and the teacher. The study would treat them as separate, independent units, as indeed was required by the statistical analysis. The nature of process involved in any change from pre- to post-test was ignored, and thus issues of causality were not addressed. Consequently, few principles relevant to classrooms could emerge.

In the same period there was little questioning of the nature of science. In particular, theorists, researchers and teachers took the content as unproblematic. Of course they recognised that some topics were more complex and difficult to learn than others, but saw teaching as essentially a matter of clarity in explanation and logical sequencing. Students would learn propositions and algorithms in the form that was presented to them. Prior knowledge would either be a benefit to understanding, or would be seen as irrelevant. It was never seen as a possible obstacle. Again no useful principles, this time about content, emerged.

The research of the 1960s did not produce principles. For science education to progress, there had to be a change in style. Certainly in the 1970s the quantity of research increased markedly. A comparison of the review of science education research by Watson (1963) in the first edition of the *Handbook of Research on Teaching* with those in the second edition by Shulman and Tamir (1973) and the third by White and Tisher (1986), and with the numerous chapters in the *Handbook of Research on Science Teaching and Learning* (Gabel 1994), reveals a surge in the amount, richness and diversity of research. However, energy in research, though welcome, is not an end in itself. To judge whether there has been progress in science education, we should look at the *style* of research. Has it changed in ways that appear more likely to create principles which are useful guides to practice? Then, have any such principles appeared? Third, what evidence is there that the research has influenced classroom practice?

White (1997; in press) analysed the shifts between 1965 and 1995 in research style, and concluded that the change in style amounted to a revolution. There had been a marked shift from interventionist studies, in which the researcher imposed an experimental form of teaching, often in artificial circumstances, to descriptive ones, where the researcher made observations over lengthy periods of time of events in working classrooms. This shift involved much greater reliance on qualitative data, and the verbatim reporting of teachers' and students' words rather than means of scores on tests. Naturally there was an accompanying move from reporting of sophisticated inferential statistics to simple descriptive statistics or no statistics at all.

The revolution was a consequence of three perceptions. One was that mechanisms of causation had to be elicited. Where earlier researchers were content, in the main, to record that a method of teaching led to certain outcomes with only mild speculation about why that happened, later ones became much more interested in how the effect occurred. This perception led them to investigate teachers' and students' epistemologies of teaching and learning, and of science. A special issue of the *Journal of Research in Science Teaching* (1991, 28 (9)) concentrated on this.

The second perception was that research needed to produce principles relevant to the practice of teaching. Teachers had little interest or faith in the conclusions from studies in psychology laboratories. Nor did brief, artificial interventions in classrooms impress them, for they knew classrooms to be complex places where a change needed time to bed down before its outcomes could be relied upon.

Researchers recognition of teachers' perspectives encouraged them to attend to ecological validity in their studies. They ceased to treat the 'subjects' in their research as puppets, and began to listen to what they had to say about what was going on. Teachers emerged first as partners and then as principals in research. It may be that this will occur with students at some time.
The third perception was that content mattered. In most studies from the 1960s, content is no more than a necessary vehicle. In comparisons of the effectiveness of teaching methods, students had to learn something, and one topic was as good as another. The research on alternative conceptions destroyed that comfortable assumption. Students' beliefs affect what they learn from instruction, and beliefs are content-specific. Content emerged as an important variable.

Analysis
The extract shows the change in emphasis in science education research. Studies from the 1960s treated pupils as individual 'subjects' to which pre-test and post-test values could be attributed. This approach lends itself to ease of statistical analysis but not to the production of usable principles to improve classroom practice.

Later research developed, with the researchers spending time in classrooms, listening to teachers and pupils and using qualitative data. This was due to a development in thinking which placed the epistemology of learning and teaching at the centre. In addition, it becomes obvious from the extract that teachers themselves felt uneasy with both psychological and statistical studies and those based on the output of visiting academics.

Finally, the extract brings us the point where teachers, in classrooms, have become principal researchers. Elsewhere in this text evidence is drawn from research programmes carried out principally by teachers. The extract also points to the importance of beliefs, or attitudes, and how these can impact on learning.

Personal response

Think back to your first teaching experience. What situation(s) would you think action research could address with the aim of improving learning?

Practical implications and activities

As a scientist and a teacher you will be aware of your need to develop subject knowledge, which you did mainly prior to starting your teacher training, and pedagogic knowledge, which you develop during your training. By selecting a topic from either the Key Stage 3 or 4 scheme of work, identify the subject knowledge and pedagogic knowledge required to deliver the material.

Why is it important, in your view, for science teachers (and others) to research the development of pedagogic knowledge?

How

If you have read Hoult (2005, Chapter 11), you will be aware of the six principles that Hopkins (2002) offers for a strong basis for teacher-led research. It is not within the scope of this text to discuss all of these principles, neither is it within the scope of this text to take the reader through the various research methodologies available to teacher researchers. These issues can be better addressed through the further reading at the end of the chapter. However it is possible, we argue, to present a beginner's model of action research based on four stages. This model is shown in Figure 11.1.

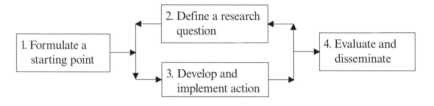

Figure 11.1 A model of action research

Stage 1 involves thinking of a general idea to investigate, for example: 'My students see physics as boring and irrelevant; how can I make it more engaging?' Stage 2 requires the researcher to pose a question, for example: 'Will teaching physics through the context of sport and music better engage my students?' Stage 3 requires the implementation of some action, for example teaching mechanics through the medium of sport and teaching light and sound through the medium of a rock concert. Stage 4 requires some evaluation of the outcomes and, as with any research, the findings need to be disseminated.

Whilst not giving details of how to collect evidence or how to evaluate outcomes, we will mention three points which all researchers should consider when planning an intervention of this nature:

- Reliability: would your chosen method of data collection produce similar results if administered again? For example, if a test is being used, would it always give similar scores for the class, or would two researchers come to the same conclusion when applying your criteria to the analysis of an interview? If

we do not have reliable data we cannot have confidence in the results.
- Validity: does the instrument used to collect data measure what you think it does? For example, does your test of chemistry measure understanding in chemistry or understanding of language?
- Ethics: are the risks (to pupils' education) outweighed by the potential benefits of the intervention? Do you have consent to expose pupils to the intervention? These are two vital questions to address before undertaking research with your pupils.

Personal response

Think about a new teaching scheme which it is hoped will increase pupils' success at GCSE by at least two grades. In what way could a test of the new scheme be considered unethical?

Practical implications and activities

Working with a colleague or your school-based mentor, plan a small-scale action research project using the four stages given above. What is your question to investigate? How will you collect data? What method of evaluation and dissemination will you employ? How have you addressed reliability, validity and ethical concerns?

Further reading

Altrichter, H., Posch, P. and Somekh, B. (1993) *Teachers Investigate their Work.* London: Routledge.

Cohen, l., Manion, L. and Morrison, K. (2000) *Research Methods in Education* (5th edition). London: Routledge.

Hopkins, I. (2002) *A Teacher's Guide to Classroom Research* (3rd edition). Buckingham: Open University Press.

Reiss, M. (2000) *Understanding Science Lessons.* Buckingham: Open University Press.

References

ACCAC (2000) *Science in the National Curriculum in Wales.* Available at http://www.accac.org.uk/eng/content.php?cID=3&pID=15 [accessed March 2006].

Adey, P. (1988) 'Cognitive Acceleration: Review and prospects', *International Journal of Science Education*, 10 (2), 121–134.

Adey, P. (1997) 'It all Depends on the Context Doesn't It? Searching for General Educable Dragons', *Students in Science Education*, 29, 45–92.

Adey, P. and Shayer, M. (1994) *Really Raising Standards.* London: Routledge.

Adey, P., Shayer, M. and Yates, C. (1995) *Thinking Science: The Curriculum Materials of the CASE Project.* London: Thomas Nelson and Sons.

Ainscow, M., Farrell, P., Tweddle, D. and Malki, G. (1999) 'The Role of LEAs in Developing Inclusive Policies and Practices', *British Journal of Special Education*, 26 (3) 136–140.

Assessment Reform Group (1999) *Assessment for Learning – Beyond the Black Box.*

Association for Science Education (1996) *Safeguards in the School Laboratory.* Hatfield: ASE.

Association for Science Education (1999) *Safe and Exciting Science.* Hatfield: ASE.

Ausubel, D.P. (1960) 'The Use of Advance Organisers in the Learning and Retention of Meaningful Verbal Material', *Journal of Educational Psychology*, 51, 267–272.

Basic Skills Agency (1997) *Does Numeracy Matter? Evidence from the National Child Development Study on the impact of poor numeracy on adult life.* London: Basic Skills Agency.

Blagg, N., Ballinger, M. and Gardner, R. (1988) *Somerset Thinking Skills Course Handbook.* Oxford: Basil Blackwell.

Blandford, S. (2003) *Professional Development Manual.* London: Pearson.

Bloom, B.S. (1956) *Taxonomy of Educational Objectives. Handbook 1: The Cognitive Domain.* London: Longmans Green.

Booth, T. and Ainscow, M. (2002) *Index for Inclusion: developing learning and participation in schools.* Bristol: CSIE.

Booth, T., Ainscow, M., Black-Hawkins, K., Vaughan, M. and Shaw, L. (2000) *Index for Inclusion: developing learning and participation in schools.* Bristol: CSIE.

Borrows, P. (1998) 'Safety in Science Education', in Ratcliffe, M. *ASE Guide to Secondary Science Education.* Hatfield: The Association for Science Education.

Brichenco, P., Johnston, J. and Sears, J. (2000) 'Children's Attitude to Science: beyond the men in white coats', in Sears, J. and Sorensen, P. *Issues in Science Teaching.* London: Routledge.

Brooks, V. (2004) 'Using Assessment for Formative Purposes, in Brooks, V, Abbott, I. and Bills, L. *Preparing to Teach in Secondary Schools*. Berkshire: Open University Press.

Case, R. (1991) *The Mind's Staircase: Exploring the underpinnings of children's thought and conceptual knowledge*. Hillsdale N.J.: Lawrence Erlbaum.

CLEAPSS (2000) Student Safety Sheets. Brunel University: CLEAPSS.

Cohen, L., Manion, L. and Morrison, K. (2000) *Research Methods in Education*. London: Routledge.

(COSHH) The Control of Substances Hazardous to Health (2002) Available at: http://www.hse.gov.uk/coshh/ [accessed March 2006].

Cunningham, H.A. (1946) 'Lecture Demonstrations versus Laboratory Method in Science Teaching', *Science Education*, 30, 70–82.

De Bono, E. (1976) *Teaching Thinking*. London: Maurice Temple Smith.

Denny, M. and Chennell, F. (1986) 'Science Practicals: What do pupils think?', *European Journal of Science Education*, 8, 325–336.

DES (1982) *Science in Schools, Age 15*. Report No 1. London: HMSO.

DES (1985) *Science 5-16: A statement of policy*. London: HMSO.

DES (1989) *Science at Age 13: A review of APU survey findings 1980-1984*. London: HMSO.

DfEE (1999) *The National Curriculum for England: Science*. London: DfEE.

DfEE (2000) *The Role of the Local Education Authority in School Education*. London: DfEE.

DfEE (2002) *Qualifying to Teach*. London: DfEE.

DfES *Pedagogy and Practice: Teaching and Learning in Secondary Schools. Unit 15: Using ICT to enhance learning*. Available at: http://publications.teachernet.gov.uk/ [accessed March 2006].

DfES Standards website available on: http://www.standards.dfes.gov.uk/keystage3/respub/scienceframework/planning/sample_lesson/ [accessed March 2006].

DfES (2001) *Special Educational Needs Code of Practice*. London: DfES.

DfES (2001) *Framework for Teaching Mathematics: Years 7, 8 and 9*. London: DfES.

DfES (2002) *The Distribution of Resources to Support Inclusion*. London: DfES.

DfES (2002) *Framework for Teaching Science: Years 7, 8 and 9*. London: DfES.

DfES (2002) *Qualifying to Teach: Professional Standards for Qualified Teacher Status and Requirements for Initial Teacher Training*. London: TTA.

DfES (2002) *Key Stage 3 National Strategy: Assessment in Science*, London: DfES.

DfES (2002) *Literacy in Science: Resource pack for participants*. Key Stage 3 National Strategy. London: DfES.

DfES (August 2004) Press Statement by David Milliband. Available at: http://www.standards.dfes.gov.uk/primary/features/literacy/984187/ [accessed March 2006].

DfES (2004) *The Science National Curriculum for England*. London: DfES/QCA.

DfES (2006) Available from National Curriculum on-line at http://www.nc.uk.net/

webdav/servlet/XRM?Page/@id=6001&POS[@stateId_eq_main]/
@id=10682&POS[@stateId_eq_note]/@id=10682 [accessed March 2006].

Driver, R. (1983) *The Pupil as Scientist?* Milton Keynes: Open University Press.

Driver, R., Leach, J., Millar, R. and Scott, P. (1996) *Young People's Images of Science.* Buckingham: Open University Press.

Education Guardian (24 January 2006) 'Children are Less Able Than They Used to Be'. Manchester: Guardian Newspaper.

Edwards, J. (1991) 'The Direct Teaching of Thinking Skills', in Evans, G. (ed.) *Learning and Teaching Cognitive Skills.* Hawthorn, Victoria: Australian Council for Educational Research.

Elliott, J. (1991) *Action Research for Educational Change.* Buckingham: Open University Press.

Elton Report (1989) *Discipline in Schools: Report of the Committee of Enquiry Chaired by Lord Elton.* London: HMSO.

Everington (2004).

Feuerstein, R. Rand, Y., Hoffman, M.B. and Miller, R. (1980) *Instrumental Enrichment: An intervention programme for cognitive modifiability.* Baltimore: University Park Press.

Foulds, K. and Gott, R. (1988) 'Structuring Investigations in the Science Curriculum', *Physics Education*, 23, 347–351.

Fullick, P.L. and Ratcliffe, M. (eds) (1996) *Teaching Ethical Aspects of Science.* Totton: Bassett Press.

Gardner, H. (1984) *Frames of Mind.* London: Heinemann.

Gaud, C.F. (1982) 'The Scientific Attitude and Science Education: A critical reappraisal', *Science Education*, 66, 109–121.

Gibson, S. and Blandford, S. (2005) *Managing Special Educational Needs. A Practical Guide for Primary and Secondary Schools.* London: Sage.

Gott, R. and Duggan, S. (1995) *Investigative Work in the Science Curriculum.* Milton Keynes: Open University Press.

Halford, G.S. (1992) *Children's Understanding: The development of mental models.* Hillsdale N.J.: Lawrence Erlbaum.

Hayden, C. and Dunne, S. (2001) *Outside, Looking In: Children's and families' experiences of exclusion from school.* London: The Children's Society.

Health and Safety Executive Statistics (1991/1992). Cited in ASE (1996) *Safeguards in the School Laboratory.* Hatfield: ASE.

Heater, D. (1999) *What is Citizenship?* Cambridge: Polity Press.

HMI (1979) *Aspects of Secondary Education.* London: HMSO.

Hodson, D. (1990) 'A Critical Look at Practical Work in School Science', *School Science Review*, 70 (256), 33–40.

Hodson, D. (1992) 'Redefining and Reorienting Practical Work in School Science', *School Science Review*, 73 (264), 65–78.

Hopkins, D. (2002) *A Teacher's Guide to Classroom Research* (3rd edition). Buckingham: Open University Press.

Inhelder, B. and Piaget, J. (1958) *The Growth of Logical Thinking*. London: Routledge.

Ireson, G.P. (2005) 'Einstein and the Nature of Thought Experiments', *School Science Review*, 86 (317), 47–53.

Kallinson, J.M. (1986) 'Effects of Lesson Organisation on Achievement', *American Educational Research Journal*, 23 (2), 337–347.

Kelly, G.A. (1970) 'A Brief Introduction to Personal Construct Theory', in Bannister, D. (ed.) *New Perspectives in Personal Construct Theory*. London: Academic Press.

Kemmis, S. (1983) 'Action Research', in Husen, T. and Postlethwaite, T. *International Encyclopedia of Education: Research and Studies*. Oxford: Permagon.

Kitson, A. (2004) 'Citizenship', in Brooks, V., Abbott, I. and Bill, L. (eds) *Preparing to Teach in Secondary Schools*. Berkshire: Open University Press.

Kuhn, T. (1963) *The Structure of Scientific Revolutions*. Chicago: University of Chicago Press.

Lawton, D. (1989) *Education, Culture and the National Curriculum*. London: Hodder.

Lewis, R. (1984) *How to Help Learners to Assess their Progress*. London: Council for Educational Technology.

Lipman, M., Sharp, M. and Oscanyan, F. (1980) *Philosophy in The Classroom*. Philadelphia: Temple University Press.

Mahoney, M.J. (1979) 'Psychology of the Scientist', *Social Studies Science*, 9, 349–375.

Management of Health and Safety at Work Regulations (1992). Available at: http://www.opsi.gov.uk/si/si1992/Uksi_19922051_en_1.htm [accessed March 2006].

Management of Health and Safety at Work Regulations (1999). Available at: www.hse.gov.uk/pubns/hsc13.pdf [accessed March 2006].

Martin, A. (1990) *Claudia and the Great Search*. New York: Scholastic.

McGuinness, C. (1999) *From Thinking Skills to Thinking Classrooms*. Nottingham: DfEE Publications.

Miller, G.A. (1956) 'The Magic Number Seven, Plus or Minus Two: Some limits on our capacity for processing information', *Psychological Review*, 63, 81–97.

Mittler, P. (2000) *Working Towards Inclusive Education*. London: David Fulton.

Monk, M. and Dillon, J. (2000) 'The Nature of Scientific Knowledge', in Monk, M. and Osborne, J. (eds) *Good Practice in Science Teaching*. Buckingham: Open University Press, 78–81.

NCR (1995) 'US National Science Education Standards'. Available at: http://newton.nap.edu/html/nses/ [accessed March 2006].

Nicholls, J. and Turner, T. (1998) 'Differentiation and Special Educational Needs', in Turner, T. and Dimarco, W. *Learning to Teach Science in Secondary School*. London: Routledge.

Nind, M. and Sheehy, K. (2004) *Inclusive Education: Learners and Learning Contexts*. London: Routledge.

Nuffield Foundation (1966) *Nuffield Chemistry: Introduction and Guide*. Harmondsworth: Longman.

Ofsted (2001) *Inspecting Mathematics 11–16 with Guidance on Self Evaluation.* London: Ofsted.

Ofsted (2003) *Good Assessment Practice in Science.* London: Ofsted.

Ofsted (2005) *Managing Challenging Behaviour.* London: Ofsted. Available at: www.ofsted.gov.uk [accessed March 2006].

Paivio, A. (1990) *Mental Representations: a dual coding approach.* Oxford: Oxford University Press.

Parkinson, J. (1994) *The Effective Teaching of Secondary Science.* Harlow: Longman.

Peterson, S., Williams, J. and Sorensen, P. (2000) 'Science for All: the challenge of inclusion', in Sears, J. and Sorensen, P. *Issues in Science Teaching.* London: Routledge.

Piaget. J. (1972). *The Child's Conception of the World.* Towota, N.J.: Littlefield Adams (original work published 1926).

Provision and Use of Work Equipment Regulations (1998). Available at: www.hse.gov.uk/pubns/indg291.pdf [accessed March 2006].

QCA (1998) *Education for Citizenship and the Teaching of Democracy in Schools.* London: QCA.

QCA (2001) *Citizenship: Scheme of Work for KS3 Teacher's Guide.* London: QCA.

QCA (2006) 'Science Programme of Study'. Available at: http://www.qca.org.uk/downloads/10340_science_prog_of_study_from_2006_ks4.pdf [accessed March 2006].

Ramsden, J.M. (1998) 'Mission Impossible?: Can Anything be Done About Attitudes to Science?', *International Journal of Science Education,* 20, 125–137.

Rapport, R. (1970) 'Three Dilemmas in Action Research', *Human Relations,* 23, 1–11.

Ratcliffe, M. and Grace, M. (2003) *Science Education for Citizenship.* Berkshire: Open University Press.

Riding, R. (2002) *School Learning and Cognitive Style.* London: David Fulton Publishers.

Ritchie, S.M. and Edwards, J. (1996) 'Creative Thinking Instruction for Aboriginal Children', *Learning and Instruction,* 6, 59–75.

Roden, J. (2005) *Achieving QTS. Reflective Reader: Primary Science.* Chapters 3 and 4. Exeter: Learning Matters.

Roopchand, G. (1987) *The Systems Model and Instructional Design and Development – a Study of Guyana.* University of Wales: PhD Dissertation.

Roopchand, G. and Moss, D. (1988) 'A Systematic Approach to the Design of Secondary School Lessons in Guyana', *British Journal of Educational Technology,* 16 (1), 43–52.

Ross, K., Lakin, L. and Callaghan, P. (2000) *Teaching Secondary Science.* London: David Fulton.

Sadler, D.R. (1989) 'Formative Assessment and the Design of Instructional Systems', *Instructional Science,* 18, 119–44.

Satterly, D. (1994) 'Quality in External Assessment', in Hralen, W. *Enhancing Quality in Assessment*. London: Paul Chapman.

Screen, P. (1986) 'The Warwick Process Science Project', *School Science Review*, 68 (242), 12–16.

Scruggs, T. and Mastropieri, M. (1996) 'Teacher Perceptions of Mainstreaming/Inclusion, 1958–1995: a research synthesis', *Exceptional Children,* 63 (1), 59–74.

Shayer, M. (1996) *The Long-term Effects of Cognitive Acceleration on Pupils' School Achievement*. London: King's College Department for Education and Professional Studies.

Shayer, M. (1999) 'Cognitive Acceleration through Science Education II: Its effects and scope', *International Journal of Science Education*, 21, (8), 883–902.

Shayer, M. (2000) *GCSE 1999: Added Value from Schools Adopting the CASE Intervention*. London: King's College Department for Education and Professional Studies.

Shayer, M. and Adey, P. (1981) *Towards a Science of Science Teaching*. London: Heinemann.

Shayer, M. and Adey, P. (2002) *Learning Intelligence*. Buckingham: OUP.

SMP (1976) *Calculators in Schools*. London: Schools Mathematics Project.

Solomon, J. (1980) *Teaching Children in the Laboratory*. London: Croom Helm.

Spens Report (1938) *Report of the Consultative Committee on Secondary Education with Special Reference to Grammar Schools and Technical High Schools*. London: HMSO.

Stenhouse, L. (1984) 'Artistry and Teaching: The teacher as a focus of research and development', in Hopkins, D. and Wideen, M. *Alternative Perspectives on School Improvement*. Lewes: Falmer Press.

Tawney, D. (1981) 'Accidents in School Laboratories: A report of an investigation', *Education in Science*, 95, 32–33.

Thompson Report (1918) *Report on Natural Science in Education*. London: HMSO.

Torrance, H. and Pryor, J. (1998) *Investigating Formative Assessment: Teaching, Learning and Assessment in the Classroom*. Buckingham: Open University Press.

Twidle, J., Childs, A., Dussart, M., Godwin, J. and Sorensen, P. (2005) *Exploring the Elements that Make an Effective Web-based Science Lesson*. British Education Communications and Technology Authority (Becta) on behalf of the Department for Education and Skills. Available at: http://www.becta.org.uk/research/research.cfm?section=1&id=4821 [accessed March 2006].

UNESCO (1994) *The Salamanca Statement and Framework for Action on Special Needs*. Paris: UNESCO.

Vygotsky, L. (1978) *Mind in Society: The Development of Higher Order Processes*. Cambridge, Mass.: Harvard University Press.

Wellington, J.J. (1986) *Controversial Issues in the Curriculum*. London: Blackwell.

White, J. (1998) *Do Howard Gardner's Multiple Intelligences Add Up?* London: Institute of Education, University of London.

Wood, D.J., Bruner, J.S., and Ross, G. (1976) 'The Role of Tutoring in Problem Solving', *Journal of Child Psychology and Psychiatry*, 17 (2), 89–100.

Woolnough, B. (1991) *Practical Science*. Milton Keynes: Open University Press.

Woolnough, B. and Alsopp, T. (1985) *Practical Work in Science*. Cambridge: Cambridge University Press.

Index

spiritual, moral and cultural development 91–2
standards 95–6, 99, 101
strategies
    for teaching and learning 49–56
structure of lessons 8
summative assessment 33, 35, 38, 40–41
support, differentiation 29
synthesis 10

tasks, differentiation 29
taxonomy, learning objectives 9–10
teachers
    and action research 105, 107, 108–9
    and inclusion 25–6
    understanding of the nature of science 78–85
teaching schemes *see* schemes of work (SoW)
tests 38, 40–41
theory 77
Thinking Science 100–1
thinking skills 97–102

thought experiments 72

understanding 10

VAK (visual, auditory and kinaesthetic) experiences
    20, 22
values 88
Vygotsky, L.S. 98, 101

WALT (we are learning today) 8–9
Wellington, J. 66–7, 78–80
White, J. 17–18
White, R. 105
WILF (what I am looking for) 8–9
working memory 15–16, 19

Yates, Carolyn 98, 101

Zone of Proximal Development (ZPD) 10